A Better TOMORROW

Veronica M Liburd

A Better Tomorrow

Authored by Veronica M Liburd

© Veronica M. Liburd 2025

Edited by Marcia M Publishing House Editorial Team

Cover design, printing & binding: Marcia M Publishing House Ltd.

Published by Marcia M Spence of Marcia M Publishing House Ltd.

On behalf of Veronica M Liburd In West Bromwich, West Midlands the UNITED KINGDOM B71.

All rights reserved 2025 Veronica M Liburd

Veronica M Liburd asserts the moral right to be identified as the author of this work. The opinions expressed in this published work are those of the author and do not reflect the opinions of Marcia M Publishing House or its editorial team.

This book is sold subject to the conditions it is not, by way of trade or otherwise, lent, hired out or otherwise circulated in any form of binding or cover other than that in which it is published. No part of this publication may be reproduced, stored in a retrieval system or transmitted in any form or by any means (electronic, mechanical, photocopying, recording or otherwise) without prior written permission from the Author.

ISBN: 978-1-0681515-3-8

A copy of this publication is legally deposited in The British Library.

www.marciampublishing.com

Dedication

To my darling love of my life.
To Mama and Daddy
Rest in Peace, My beloveds

My girls and my grandchildren

I would like to thank my daughters, Crystal, and Marsha who helped me throughout this time of grieving Carlos's passing. Throughout this difficult, crucial time, you both were my rock by holding me with kindness and empathy. This helped me through the emptiness, loneliness and confused time I endured. Sabrina and the children weren't present at that time but Sabrina came to the funeral to pay her respects. I'm so thankful for my Heavenly Father, who didn't leave me alone during this hurtful, endurable time. I felt the tender loving care and love you gave me, my daughters and my three grandchildren. I will always be thankful for your thoughtful and love towards me.

To God be the glory for all He has done from the inside out of my being. Great things He has done and what He is still doing in my life.

ACKNOWLEDGMENTS

My Dear Friends

I would like to thank my friend, who has been by my side from school, through thick and thin, Ava. We have known each other for 63 years. Our lives have been a roller coaster but we have always been able to smile at the storms and give each other the space to live and strive through our storms of life. Not knowing when we will see each other again, it could be years later, but with the understanding we would have each other's back no matter what and catch up with what has happened from the last visit. We have strong shoulders to bear each other's burdens, no matter what comes our way. We live near each other now, which helps us to check each other twice or more a week, which is great. God is and always is on His throne always. I always remind us both of God's grace and love towards us.

My dear friends Pricella

My other friend is Pricella, who has also been my rock for 37years. Pricella accepted me when I felt unsure and being around difficult people, who weren't very friendly, which brought up the feeling, again not being good enough, which was very difficult. Pricella was the one who showed me kindness and acceptance. She saw me as a very shy person who wanted to better my life for my family and myself. Her profession as a midwife helped me with Sabrina, when she was born 10yrs after Marsha. She was a blessing to me and I will always thank her for her time, kindness and patience towards me and Sabrina. We are also friends to this day.

My other dear friend Violet

Violet was the other friend who I felt was very genuine and was very shy and we both understood each other. We both were in a similar situation and became friends. Violet is Sabrina god mother and always acknowledged this role. Violet would take time to speak to Sabrina, bought her something for her birthday and Christmas without fail and made sure her godchild was ok. I always will appreciate those precious times she was present, helpful through some difficult times in my life. We became very close, even up to this day. I will always appreciate her for who she is kind**.**

Maryanne - I acknowledged when we attended the CPCAB Level 4 Diploma in Therapeutic Counselling course for two years. The course was intense, bringing up issues that had been dormant. We were drawn to each other within the group. We created a very close relationship, which helped us through very difficult times. We were split into small groups where we had to work together. We had to face emotional issues. This caused us to create a confide relationship throughout the years until today. I appreciate and thank her for being a true friend.

Blake - introduced by a family member.

We would invite him to any celebrations we had. We all accept him and his two children. Blake is a very sincere and a kind person. He loves his family and his children, Grace. (9) and Thomas (10). He doesn't think twice about teaching his children and my grandchildren to ride a bike in the back street or taking the three of them to the park or climbing. The three children enjoy each other's company. Blake loved seeing them enjoying and experiencing new topics. He offers to help if I ever need anything. Throughout the loss of Carlos, Blake offered his time and kept a close eye on me. One Morning out of the blue, he called and asked if I would like to have breakfast. I was touched by this random gesture of kindness. Another time I was going away for a few days and out of the blue he offered to take me to the coach station and collect me when I arrived back. I was overwhelmed. We can speak about anything and he accepts me as his second mum. There are so many reasons why I acknowledge him as a very special person in my life, as **my son**.

Logan – I have known for years.

Logan has also been very caring, kind and attentive. The Christmas after losing Carlos, I started looking at Carlos's picture. I missed him so much, my heart ponding so fast, I started holding my chest. I couldn't stop crying.

I have not felt so much pain since my dear mother's passing. I felt so deflated, so small, just like a little girl with no one to help me. I felt like an orphan, not belonging to anyone. I felt so lost, alone in this room. All of a sudden the door opened and Logan appeared, founding me in floods of tears, crying and deflated. Without knowing Logan was keeping a close eye on me. Everyone came into the room at this point to make sure I was ok. I will always be grateful for his sensitivity and attentiveness to me.

My Brother and Sister in Christ

There are two precious people I can never forget is Lucas and Hanna. The support and encouragement they showed me during the times of hardship and sorrow. I value them as my brother and sister. We treat each other as family. In my time of hardship and distress, they helped me in so many ways, by praying and encouraging me. This strengthened my spiritual muscles. I was blessed by these two people, whom I admired and thank for their kindness, support in helping me with my confidence, to move forward. They never made me feel inadequate or not good enough. They always reassured me it would be ok and continued to pray for me. Lucas is very wise and knowledgeable in the faith and would always reflect on God's words and promises. His passion for God just seeps through him with kindness, truth and comforting words. They both are truthly my brother and sister in Christ. Lucas would be honest even when I found it hard to hear the truth. We have never had a word of disenchantment or a word of upset. I just want to celebrate them and thank them for being such great friends to me and my family. We have been friends for over 40years and we are still the same with each other today.

My Adopted Sons and Daughter

I would like to mention Cameron, who is the father of my eldest granddaughter Violet and grandson Tristin, who are Crystal's children.

I have always seen Cameron and Julianna as my son and daughter. They have never been disrespectful. We all communicate with each other often to make sure we are ok. The two of them have been kind, acknowledging and attentive towards me. Our relationships are a son and daughter demeanour.

In Memory of My Beloved Grandmother

Forgiveness Is The Key That Releases Pain, Sorrow, Abandonment and Fear and Also Brings True Peace, Freedom and Happiness

Everyone who is mentioned in this book has helped me to grow in maturity, into who I am today. They influenced my life to progress into a woman of substance, empowerment and forgiveness to stand steadfast in all I have achieved. The journey was not easy, full of challenges, fears of the unknown but pushing through to gain **A Better Tomorrow**. Being taught by my dear **Mother** to hold on to the hand which will never let me go, my **Creator, Saviour and Lord** who never abundant me but held me steadfast on **his promises**.

Thank you, god for all the experiences. I understand it more now; help me to always acknowledge you in all I do.

Contents

Dedication iii
Acknowledgments v
The Worst News Of My Entire Life 1
The Beginning of Losing My Innocence 9
Secondary School for Girls 15
My first Boyfriend Daniel 20
Leaving School 25
Self 31
First Marriage 38
Dangerous Times 53
Carlos Again 63
The Accident 68
Frightened 74
Returning to Work 76
Teach Me Hairdressing 79
Second Marriage 93
Change Has Come 107
Wake-up Call 120
Work Hard Play Hard 129
Gold Chain and Anchor 137
From Paradise to Reality 142
Mama Going into The Home 151
My Father's Funeral 155

Taking It Slow	163
Becoming a Registered Centre	169
Love and Care	175
The Change	188
Forgiveness	193
Is Love Not Enough?	195
My Darling Carlos	200
About The Author	207

1
THE WORST NEWS OF MY ENTIRE LIFE

"Where am I going? I don't know her. I don't want to go; grandma!" I felt the tears rolling down my face and into my mouth. I couldn't stop crying. "Why have I got to leave you and aunty, grandma? I don't know my mother or father." Even though my grandma told me about my mother, I still thought my grandma was my mom, and I felt so abandoned. I felt like I had done something wrong. It felt like I was being given away.

I was frightened; my heart was pounding, and it hurt. It was like my body was screaming from inside, I didn't understand why and continued to cry. It was a feeling that overwhelmed me, an all-encompassing feeling of abandonment and rejection.

"Grandma, I don't want to leave you and aunty, please I don't want to go, Grandma, don't make me go away please!"

My grandmother, who everyone called Doota, had white hair and darkish skin. She was very loving, gentle, and I felt she loved me very much. I had lived with Grandma and my aunty my whole life in Gingerland, Nevis, where I was born in 1955. My aunty, Virginia on the other hand, seemed to be very quiet in the background. I used to play in a very large open space; it was a large field that went on and on. There were a lot of fruit trees, although I didn't know what they were. All I know is I used to pick the fruits, wash and eat them. Thinking of my grandmother's house, the only room I remember specifically had a cabinet with glasses of different shapes and sizes and a key in the lock. I remember this room because it was in this room that my grandmother told me the worst news of my entire life. "You're leaving us, Ronnie, and going to England to live with your mother." I remember the open brown door as she propped herself up, stretching her arm to the top, to balance herself. I sensed fear as I became very warm inside and outside my body.

The first memory I have was at five or six years old. I accidentally stepped on a piece of hot coal, which was in the garden. I remember screaming and wailing and holding my foot as it swelled, I could feel the pounding and pain. It was excruciating. Everyone was concerned and my aunty and grandmother attended to me. My grandmother said, "Keep still, darling." I was in so much pain, but that's what I remember, my grandmother's tender, loving voice.

My grandmother continued telling me to look after Emma because she is younger than you. "I want you to be a good girl." She said, "You may not see me again."

"Oh, why won't I see you again?"

"Because your mum wants you with her. She will look after you and you will have to look after Emma because she is going to England to her mother, too."

My next memory was of seeing a large ship. And then we were walking on these wooded steps, with a rope for a handle, called a gangway. I remember feeling scared. This person who was holding Emma's hand was very caring. Whilst I had to hold on to the rope on my own. I remember hanging on for dear life, as these wooden steps were moving so much and I had to keep walking.

I was very frightened, thinking I'm going to fall. At this point, I wanted to cry but I didn't really know this woman and she may get angry with me.

I felt sick and had a terrible feeling in my stomach when I looked down at those stairs and saw the bright blue sea below. *I'm going to fall*, I thought and I will not see my grandma again. Looking down, I was so scared I just wanted this to be over.

On the ship, I was seasick all the time. The woman who was holding Emma's hand told me later she was sister Melda (my second eldest sister) and both of us were Emma's aunties.

Being left in the cabin was lonely, as I was alone most of the time. The ship was rocking to and fro. I was so scared. I wanted to go back home. I had to run into this small space and bend over the toilet to be sick. I would sit on the toilet seat most of the time because I was told by my sister not to have any accidents on the floor. I vomited so much I felt someone had hit me in my stomach. I then remembered my grandma's smiling face and kind voice and hugs. The house, the big fields. The sun, the mango trees, and the fruit trees near the house. I cried. The tears would roll down my face and into my mouth. I tasted the saltiness, which made me feel even worse.

Why was I alone in this room? It didn't feel right. I would pray for Emma and sister Melda to come back. I didn't know why I had been left in this room for so long. I wasn't told where they went. All I knew that I was left alone in this small room and didn't even think of touching the door handle to open the door. Emma didn't speak about anything she saw. Most of the time I was so frightened I would lie in bed and pray for my grandma to come and get me. Then I heard the door open. I felt excited to see Emma and get something to eat but unfortunately, I would be sick after eating anything. It seemed a lifetime being on this boat. (My mother told me later that the journey on the ship took six weeks to get to England). I remember one night I heard voices and which woke me up. It was very worrying as it made me feel frightened to hear a voice that I didn't recognise. There was a mirror on the wall that I looked into and saw my sister and another person in bed with her. I looked around at Emma; she was sleeping. I laid down and continued looking into the mirror but there was no movement like before and it was quiet and the next thing I knew, I must have fallen asleep. There was no one in the room apart from me, Emma, and my sister. So, I didn't think about this again.

I remember getting off the ship; I was freezing. I had no feeling in my hands and feet; I was shivering, steam was coming out of my mouth, I was very curious, why I was so cold. Sister Melda gave me a jacket to put on and also put a jacket on Emma and herself. I felt slightly warmer than before. Looking up at the sky, there was no moon. It was cloudy, cold, and dark. There was smoke coming out of huge buildings, and all in a long line. It was so cold that we all were shivering. My next memory was of going to one of these buildings.

It was very warm when we got inside. I could hear other children speaking. As we went into this room, there was one girl and two boys. They all looked happy and were eating biscuits and having a drink. This woman came up to me and called me by my name. "Hello Ron, you have grown into a big girl!" (not knowing this person was my eldest sister Isabella). I just smiled and said nothing. After a short time, Emma was sat down and given something to drink and this woman took off her jacket. I was looking at Emma, wondering if she was going to put her jacket back on. I then heard this woman say "ok, we will see you later" and my sister Melda and I left Emma behind.

I started to cry and asked my sister, "Why can't Emma come with us?" She told me that Emma had to stay with her mother, father and all her brothers and sister now. She held my hand and we went to this other building. She knocked on the door and a woman opened it. We went up some stairs and my sister knocked at another door and a voice answered, saying, "Come in!" In this room was a man on the bed, and a woman who stretched out her hands and said, "Come, Ma, come." She held me close, hugged me, and cried. She told me, "I'm your mother. Call me, Mama, Ronnie." I instantly liked her and felt she was kind. The man woke up with outstretched arms, "Come here, come here, I'm your father!" I could feel my eyes opening wide with fear. I didn't dare go near him. This was how I felt toward this man and felt kindness from my mother. When I saw her crying, I wanted to cry too.

In this same house we lived in, my mother used to leave me with this woman who had a lot of other children to look after. This room was downstairs. Before you entered the room, there were sounds of crying young babies and young children. As the door opened, there was a strong scent of urine and a strong smell of poo, coming from the dirty nappies. There was a fireplace that was always lit and gave out wonderful heat. There were bottles on the shelf over the fireplace. My mother told me to sit in the chair that the lady told me to sit on and don't move. I should always ask the lady first. Only move if I needed the toilet and return to the same chair I was sitting on. I obeyed my mother's wishes because I didn't want to ever disappoint her.

The next memory is of going to school and whoever took me to school also collected Emma as well. This was the first time I had seen Emma in a while.

I asked her if she liked her brothers and sister; she said nothing. As Emma was younger than me, I felt sad most of the time without her. I was still not happy with our being separated. I really felt responsible for her. I couldn't look after her like my grandmother had instructed.

After being taken to school. I took Emma to the toilet and realised she had forgotten to wear her underwear. I was so embarrassed for her. I remember telling a teacher and someone came to the school with her underwear. This made me feel I was still looking after her.

Shortly after going to school and seeing Emma every day, Mama told me we were moving into our own house but I would have to leave this school and go to another school. Again, I felt very upset because I couldn't look after Emma again or see her every day.

We moved into our house. My mum, dad and I were in this big house. The rooms were so big. There were five rooms, a big kitchen, and a cellar, which was very scary and very cold. There were coals for the fire, piled at one side, and the two meters on the far side of the next room. My mother showed me the meters by marking the gas meter, which gave us warmth, and the electric meter, which gave us light. My mother made sure I understood the difference between the two meters. Just in case the electric or gas went off and how to put the money in the meters. Just in case I was ever in the house on my own. I was thinking about how scary the cellar looked and how I would never want to go down here on my own.

Following this, my parents had tenants in the house. It was very different because I was told I had to stay out of the way when anyone was in the kitchen or in the dining room. There were quite a few different tenants who lived and left the house. Some were nice, some were not. After school I had to go to a neighbour's house until my mother came home from work. Again, I was told, sit on the chair, only move if you want the toilet, don't move until I come to collect you. As I sat there on this chair, it felt that all the people in the house were family. Their accent was unfamiliar to mine.

Whilst I waited for Mum to collect me, they were two men speaking. One of them looked at me with a smirk on his face, staring and grinning at me. I just ignored him. Then I saw his hands moving in his pockets. I'd never seen that before and it didn't feel right. As I sat there, I listened and tried to understand what they were saying.

My mind drifted to the incident that happened at school that day. I found it hard to cope, being the only black girl in the school. All I heard from them were racist names such as blacky, nigger, golly wog, flat nose, big bum. They slapped, spat, and kicked me every day. It was a nightmare. I felt so alone, unliked and sometimes I wondered, why am I here suffering each day by these horrible people? Why do they hate me so much? They are many and I'm on my own. All I ever do is cry and that didn't stop them. I noticed another black girl was in my class today; I felt a lot better to see someone else who is black, but she had a lighter skin colour than me. Today, this boy in the class started picking a fight with me. I felt so deflated and scared I didn't know what to do. The teacher said she would be a minute and went out of the classroom.

This new girl Ava stood up and said to the boy, "Let's go behind there, as she pointed to the blackboard. "Come on then," Ava said in a stern voice.

"Ok, let's go behind there then," said the boy, red faced and frowning. The blackboard had wheels on, and from the front you could see someone's feet up to their calves. All the class could see their feet shuffling around. I could see Ava jumping up and heard the boy say, "Don't hit me," he shouted. I was so frightened for her. Someone shouted, "The teacher's coming!" They both ran and sat down. I looked at her as a champion. I held her in high esteem. At break time, I asked her, "Why did you do that for me?"

"Because he's always bullying you and it's not right."

I was so sorry she wasn't here that day. Again, I was beaten by another boy who usually felt I was his punching bag. I went to the staff room again to report the incident. This time I had a bloody nose. The door opened, and the smoke that came out of the room shocked me. I was told to stop telling tales and go back out to the playground. I felt the tears rolling down my face as I tried to wipe the tears away and blow my nose. I didn't want him to see me crying. Feeling scared but not wanting him to see that. I returned to the playground. Maybe he was waiting for me to hit me again because I went to the staff room. This male teacher didn't like me, anyway. Thinking of him slapping and spitting in my face every day. Then calling me racist names. I'm sick of crying and feeling so small and smelling his dirty saliva on my face. I'm upset and sick to death of being bullied by this stupid boy every day. I'm going to tell Mama tonight about this.

The first thing I told Mama when she got home was what happened today. Mama was terribly upset and told me she couldn't go to the school the next day because she couldn't have any time off work, for fear of losing her job. Mama asked me, "Did you report this to the teachers every time anyone bullied you?" I have never seen my mother and father so upset. Ronnie, never be ashamed of who you are. "Take off you shoe and hit him with it," and he will stop hitting you. After Mum told me this, I felt a bit better, but still scared and worried about doing this, in case it didn't work. I know he's going to hit me again tomorrow. I couldn't sleep just thinking about what Mama told me and what I intended to do. Morning came quickly. I'm so scared to go to school today.

Whilst I was walking, I couldn't feel the ground. My heart was pounding. I felt it was coming out of my chest. It became worse. I had to sit on the wall to catch my breath. I took deep breaths; my mouth became dry. I started praying and asked God to take this feeling away, please.

After a few minutes, I felt better. I was almost at the school gates. I continued walking. Before I entered the gate, I prayed again, "God, please be with me today, please, Lord. I'm so scared. I pray for Ava to be in my class today to help me. Amen."

At break time, we were all outside. Then, this boy came up and slapped me in the face. I remembered my mother's voice; take off your shoe; don't be scared; beat him with it. I felt this strength and anger from my stomach rising to my chest. I took my shoe off and started hitting him with it. I chased him around the playground. I felt such a release of freedom, a sense of strength for sticking up for myself at last. I could have cried for joy. I was overwhelmed. I didn't feel defeated or ashamed. I felt a big feeling of relief and power. I will never allow anyone to disrespect me and hit me again. This boy never bothered me again. The last time I set eyes on him was when he walked past my secondary school. He saw me and crossed over to the other side of the road.

I remembered having a fever (due to chickenpox). In my teens, I dreamt of seeing my grandmother in a coffin dressed all in white. I remember feeling terrified, as I knew she must have died. I shared my parents' bedroom at the time. I got up in the night and told my mum what I had seen. She got up to make sure I was ok, then told me to stop saying silly things.

In the next few days my mum got a telegram saying that my grandmother had died the exact night when I saw my grandmother in a coffin. My mother was distraught with grief. This was the first time I saw my mother so down and unhappy. I was so upset and couldn't stop crying for weeks. My grandma meant the world to me. Knowing I wouldn't ever see Grandma again made me so sad. It took a long time before my mum and I laughed or made each other laugh; we were always mentioning how much we loved her and how much we missed her. This was one of the saddest times in both our lives and very hard to cope with. We still live with this grief to this day.

2.
THE BEGINNING OF LOSING MY INNOCENCE

There was a tenant in the house, who was family. He was the son of an older man who came to our house. I remember this elderly man. He always came to the house just before my mum cooked and didn't leave until she asked him if he wanted any dinner. Of course, the answer was always, "Yes, I do, thank you."

Now, this man looked slender, and it appeared to me he didn't eat at home, but he would come to our house to get fed. I used to tell Mama, "Why are you giving this man food all the time?" Mama would say, "It's only a bit of food, Ronnie; God will bless us. He will make a way and you never know who will help one of our family. I just saw my mother as the kindest person, and it made me feel bad for thinking in this way. I felt God was listening to me, and knowing this, I felt even worse than before. I still felt that he took advantage of my mother's kindness. My father was also upset and told my mother the exact same thing. He felt he was coming to our house for food so he could save his money. One thing about my father was that he was very honest and said what was on his mind. He didn't care, family or not.

There was a family member who used to be kind to me. He was the son of the man who used to always come and eat at our house. His son used to buy me sweets. One evening he came downstairs and told me he had some sweets upstairs in his room. As I was in the room, he started talking to me about school and how my friends were to me.

This went on for a while. He would check to see if I was all right in the kitchen as I prepared the food and then he'd return to his room. I thought nothing of the conversations we were having. He seemed very friendly and concerned.

One day, he started telling me what a nice girl I was. Slowly but surely, he invited me into his room. I felt I could trust him as he was family and not a stranger. He told me to sit near him. He started touching himself and told me he wanted me to feel something but he would not hurt me at all.

He took my hand and gently guided my hand to his private area. I was shocked and pulled away, then I rushed out of the door. I couldn't believe what had happened. I had to stop and think, am I dreaming? This can't be true. After a few days he stayed in his room when he heard me going downstairs.

Again, I was alone cooking in the kitchen; he started telling me he was sorry for frightening me and he would not do that again. He said to me, "Don't tell anyone; this is between us." Again, he talked me around to going back into his room. This time, it went further.

He told me to stand up and he went to the back of me and I felt this hard thing between my legs. I felt terrified and it felt really wrong. I then told him to let me go and told him I was going to tell my mother. I felt so dirty and ashamed that I let this happen to me. What will my mother say? She will be ashamed of me. My sisters and other people would be so ashamed of me. I decided not to tell my mother, but to stay away from this dirty man.

I told him to never speak to me again and that I was still going to tell my mother. My intention was to never ever speak to him again. I made sure I had nothing to do with him.

I didn't speak to him at any time. Then, he told my mother he was leaving shortly after. My father's reaction and my mother's disapproval worried him.

This happened twice to me again, by a cousin who should know better, I thought. This was a grown man. Jack had permission to stay the night. He came into my mum and dad's bedroom, as the door was open. Knowing they had gone to work, he told me he liked me. He would buy me anything I wanted. The thought echoing in my head came back to me. I couldn't believe this was happening to me again. I told him to get out and I will tell my mum. Shortly after, I hear the door shut. I looked out of the window and he looked up. As our eyes met, I drew back the curtain. I couldn't believe he was trying to do the same thing. The respect had gone. I told him I'm going to tell my mother, which I did. He said he was sorry and disappeared out of the room swiftly. He left without saying a word. He was not allowed to visit the house for years and every one of my family knew about it. If my father knew, he would have confronted him. My father was a man who would not only accept sorry for such behaviour. He was very resentful and disgusted by men who took advantage of any child and especially his own flesh and blood.

The next person was a family member's husband. She asked me to babysit their two children. They were three and two years old. This particular evening which was a Friday. When I arrived, were not in. Her husband let me in. As I'm going into the dining room. He grabbed me and pushed me towards the wall and started to take off my underwear. I was so frightened and afraid of what he wanted to do. I started shouting at him to stop. "What are you doing? Get off me! I'm going to tell my Mum and Dad, get off me now!" The struggle went on and he was still trying to pull his trousers zip down. I was so frightened. It seemed like he was going to overpower me.

Then I just took some deep breaths and started wriggling again and didn't stop with all of my might. I then got away and pulled my underwear up and ran as fast as I could. I was so shocked by his action. All I could think about was *God; he was going to hurt me.* I would have been about 13yrs. I started crying and didn't stop until got home.

I started shouting and screaming, telling him to let me go. I'm going to tell my Mum. The struggle went on for some time. I thought I can't let him hurt me. Please let me go. I just wanted help, but I only had myself. I said, "Don't do this. I don't want you to do this." I could feel his hand going toward his trousers and he was trying to zip his trousers down. The fear of him hurting me was so overwhelming. I just said, "Please God, help me." I started wriggling again and this time my underwear was nearly down and he had me fixed to the wall. I wriggled and eventually got away and ran out of the door, pulling my underwear up. I was crying and I ran all the way home. When I got into the house, I must have looked a mess. My father was there, and Mama. I was devastated, frightened, and very upset.

The police were called. I had to go to hospital for an examination to make sure I was still a virgin. I remembered the examination. I felt so embarrassed and ashamed. The examination was painful, and I felt degraded and a feeling of how people will feel about me now. I felt so small and dirty. This went to court. Mama told my family member to let him plead guilty and to tell the court that he is sorry, and he will never do this ever again. He had to pay a fine because of his plea. I don't really know the outcome, but Mama didn't want this to go public as she was thinking about my future.

Years later I walked into a grocery store, with Crystal about three yrs old in her pram. This man looked back and saw me and began staring at me, then looked at Crystal, looked back at me with a grin on his face. I felt very uncomfortable. (I felt he was trying to intimidate me. He paid for his purchase; he continued looking at me until he left the shop.

The next time I heard anything about him was when Crystal came home from her part-time job at the age of sixteen with her friend. This man started picking a fight with her friend whilst they were on the bus. He walked up to her friend, which appeared he was going to hurt her. Crystal would not just stand there to see her friend being beaten. She took her umbrella and beat this man until it broke on him. The next day she saw my niece and she was telling her that a young girl had hit a member of the family with an umbrella yesterday. She described this person. Then I knew who he was. Years later, I finally revealed to Crystal who the man was and what he had done to me.

These experiences have caused me to think about my own children's safety. Making them very aware of taking anything from anyone, especially if they don't feel comfortable no matter who they are. They can tell me anything at any time. It's my job to take care of them and they have to take care of themselves. I was very careful about who I really trust with them? I have always thought about all these traumas. How have these affected me in my life and relationships with men? I used to think about how I truly felt about these men and why they feel they had the right to do this to me. The first one, as a child, was out of curiosity. I remember a girl came to visit a lady tenant, and her boyfriend came with her. They started kissing and he touched her breasts and her bottom in front of me. They were much older than me. At the time, I felt really embarrassed and they didn't care. I remember seeing this girl several times after and she never looked me in the eye, always looked away. Could this be the image that was imprinted in my brain? Is this why I went back to that man's room even though I really knew I shouldn't have, because I knew it didn't feel right?

One day Mama told me, "I'm giving you a key for the house, but mind Ronnie: I'm trusting you. Don't lose it. Don't let anyone know you have a key, because they could use it to break into the house. Make sure it's at the bottom of your bag and keep your bag safe, please, Ronnie, I beg you, ok?"

"Yes, Mama, I promise."

Opening the door for the first time with "my" own key. I felt responsible and important. There was one tenant and her young son living in the house at this time. I liked this lady. She appeared to be very nice. She would always ask me, "Do you want a biscuit or a drink?"

"No thank you," I would say as my mama told me to never take anything from anyone who was not family. This lady licked her lips a lot before she spoke, which looked funny. She spoke with a high-pitched voice and was short and slightly overweight. She had black silky straight hair, which looked like Asian hair. I liked her; she saw I did a lot of work around the house and always told me; you're a very good girl". She lived at the house for some time. I overheard one day my parents speaking and my dad said, "Camila is a good woman."

My mother's response was, "Yes, she is and you have respect towards her. Remember, she is paying her rent. (At this time, I didn't know what that meant.)

A routine was set up for me. Mum taught me how to prepare the food from seven years old. I started peeling the vegetables, learning how to make West Indian soup, curry goat, and rice, saltfish, and Johny cakes and other dishes by the age of 10 years. Mum would get up at 5am and start the food for the evening. The aroma coming upstairs from the kitchen. The meat, fish, and chicken, seasoned with mum's special herbs, smelled delicious. The aroma would wake me up. I used to guess what was for dinner tonight by the wonderful smell coming up the stairs. I knew the breakfast would be the last thing Mum did before heading upstairs to get her shower and then dressed. Mum also made breakfast bacon, sausages, and beans, cereal, or porridge. Mum did all this before she went to work every morning, before leaving the house at 7.30am every morning.

My evening chores included cooking dinner and cleaning the house. By the age of 11, I was cooking and cleaning very well.

3.
SECONDARY SCHOOL FOR GIRLS

Changing schools was very exciting at first, but when I got there, I found I was put in the lowest form. I was with people who couldn't speak English. I felt so embarrassed and again ashamed. Again, being the one that was below average. Telling my mother, I felt she was very disappointed, but my father didn't help because he always made me feel I was not good enough.

Mum said it's ok Ronnie, just pray and God will help you move up higher. I had so much love for my mum; she would always encourage me to aim for the stars. At school I had Ava, who fought for me in junior school. She was always there if I needed her and eventually; we got other friends but remained close. This made me feel much better about myself. I still studied very hard but unfortunately throughout secondary school I remained in the middle set. I eventually had more friends as I became the one that everyone would come to for advice and empathy. I had a lot of friends who were Asian, as we were in the same class.

I found that people would want to talk to me and seek advice. I didn't know why but they did. I felt sometimes that others saw me as a wise individual that they trusted, as I never told other people what they shared with me. I was very loyal to all my friends. I was not pleased with being in the lowest set. I prayed and worked very hard to get to the middle set and I got there.

I volunteered to play the violin. I felt very nervous playing for the first time in assembly. Making mistakes that sounded squeaky (of course, people were chuckling, which made me feel embarrassed and shy in front of the whole school. I just kept going. At the end of the assembly, my music teacher told me I did really well. This is one thing I am still proud of, because I pushed myself to be brave, to overcome my fear of shyness and feelings of not being good enough.

This reminded me of my niece, who was older than me. She was a first-class student. She used to show off about her grades, her ability at school. Everyone in the family had her on a pedestal. Everyone was proud of her lighter skin colour. I was given the impression; I was below her by others.

In my world, there was a lot going on with my Asian friends. They were not allowed boyfriends, but after school, a lot of them met up with them. One of my Asian friends ran away and was found, and I heard she got married and was sent away. Before this happened, she came and asked me to hide her in the house. I asked my mum if we could help her, but my mum was very concerned about our own lives. Mum told her, "Sorry, but we can't allow you to stay. If your family knew we kept you here, they wouldn't be pleased, and we would be in danger. Later on, I heard they found her with a boy in Roundhay Park and they took her to Birmingham to stay with family. Unfortunately, I never saw her again. Sometimes I still think about her and wonder what really happened to her.

I remember being happy. I had my key to let myself into the house. I felt very responsible and trustworthy. I didn't miss not going to my neighbour's house or seeing that man touching himself every minute. I felt good having the house to myself. There were no tenants. It was great. I had my space to enjoy the house until my dad came home around 5.30pm.

In getting to know my friends very well, there were a few that I trusted. One day three of us were talking. "So, what do you do when you get home from school then?" I asked. "Nothing…, Ava said.

"Really? You don't do any chores after school?" I was surprised. "Why, how come?"

"Well, my dad cooks and my mum comes in later and we have our tea, watch TV, then we get ready for bed."

"So, what do you do, Isabella, when you go home?" I asked.

"Well, my mother looks after children and is at home all day, so when I get in, I watch TV and do some homework if I have any. If not, I generally read until I go to bed."

"Ok." nodding my head in disbelief. "Lauren, do you have any chores after school?"

"Not really, because my mum works part time and is at home when I get back from school. So, I usually watch TV."

"Ok, you guys are good, that you don't have chores to do."

"Well, since you've asked us all. What chores have you had to do after school? asked Ava.

"Well, when I go home, I have to tidy the house and cook before my parents come home. I have to sweep down the stairs, sweep from the front door to the dining room, then continue sweeping in the kitchen. Then wash the dishes and finish the cooking before my parents come home."

"What time do they get in from work?"

"My dad gets in between 5.30 and 6.00pm."

"No wonder you can't stay behind after school."

"Yes, if I don't finish by the time my father gets in, I'll be in so much trouble."

"Wow! You've got a lot to do. I'll come and help you if you want me to. I don't mind." said Ava.

"We can come and help you too if you want," said another girl.

"If you do, you will have to leave by 4.30pm, just in case my father gets home early. Because I'll get into terrible trouble if he finds you there. I'm serious. He will hit me."

"I really feel sorry for you, honestly, Veronica. It's sound's a lot."

"I really appreciate you all offering to help me. Well, I can put on some music when you're helping me."

This time in my life was so good, but I didn't tell my parents about it (I told my mum when I was older)

We were good girls and they all had respect for the house and all they wanted was to help me clean the house and play music and dance. One of my friends would clean the dining room, another would sweep from the door and sweep the stairs and another one would wash the dishes. I was the only one who attended to the cooking. (There were four of us). Whilst the cleaning and cooking was going on, we would take it in turns to play the gram. We would all dance as we did the chores. It was fun and this was when the stories of what was going on in school were discussed. We had a great time.

Sometimes not all of them could come, but we would make the most of it and enjoy ourselves. One afternoon, two of my friends had a dispute and an argument developed.

Ava went out of the door and Isabella wouldn't let Ava come back in. "Let me in!" shouted Ava.

"No, I will not, because you're being cheeky," said Isabella.

"Let me in. I'm not joking!" replied Ava.

"No," Isabella replied. All of a sudden, Ava said something that was not very nice and Isabella opened the door and ran after Ava down the street. I was very worried but couldn't leave the door open or do anything.

I found myself shouting, "Run, Ava! Run, Isabella!" I shouted for both of them because I knew if Isabella got hold of Ava, it wouldn't have been pleasant. And I cared for both of them. They both were athletes and excellent runners. I was concerned all night and couldn't wait to get to school. I prayed that neither of them got hurt.

The next day I spoke to Isabella, and she was very upset and told me she would get Ava at break time. I pleaded with her, "Please let me speak to Ava, because I know she didn't mean what she said and will apologise."

I talked to Ava, and she told me, "I was mad because Isabella wouldn't let me in." Ava planned to say sorry to Isabella because she knew she shouldn't have insulted her. She was going to apologise at lunch and hoped Isabella would accept it. They made it right between themselves and everything was ok again. I was very relieved because they were both my friends. That evening, they didn't come home with me. I felt that they still needed time to come to terms with what had happened.

As I was alone. I went up to the attic. Looking at the sky, it appeared that the sky was moving but I know it's the earth. Watching the clouds, I saw the shape of a dove. I felt a warmth within me and I prayed, "God, show yourself to me. I do believe and trust you. I need you to help me in everything I do. Thank you for helping my friends to apologise to each other and help them know you like I know you, Heavenley Father. I know you hear my prayers and you will answer them in your own time. I love and thank you Father, Amen."

I have always believed that there is a God who created me in his own image, who holds me in his arms through hard times, when I do and say the wrong things or think badly of others. I'm aware of my thoughts so I will not go against God's wishes. Showing empathy, kindness, and love to others. Allows me to learn and demonstrates God's love for me so I can pass on the same love to others. Going to church every week with Mum. Allows me to be more grounded in God. He will never leave me nor forsake me but will always be in the midst of all things. God will always guide me on the best path so I can gain the victory. I had my confirmation, which meant a lot to me. In taking holy communion, I really saw this as being consecrated to God.

4

My first Boyfriend Daniel

My first boyfriend was a boy I knew. Our two families got on very well and were very close. He used to carry my books from school. We would avoid the main street, as there may be people on buses who possibly knew our parents. He walked me nearby my house. I guess we fell in love, and kept this walking was very fruitful for us. This was our special moment for two years. We would kiss goodbye and that was as far as it went.

He knew the house and where my bedroom was. One night, I felt a cold hand around my mouth. To my amazement, it was him. "What are you doing? How did you get in?"

"Through the window in the bathroom."

"How did you know it wasn't locked?"

"I didn't I just tried the window and I realised it wasn't locked."

"Why did you do this? What do you think I am? Who do you take me for? This is not right. Suppose my parents wake up. How bad would this look? They would think I'm part of all this. Just leave before any of them wake up. You know how my father is. Please, just go. Please, just go please before they come in please I'm begging you, please just go," I started crying. I was so overwhelmed and very upset.

"Oh, ok," he said.

"Get out, go out how you came in. It's not fair on me, just go." I had to speak very quietly so I didn't wake up my parents. I was so angry and scared. Oh God, if any of my parents came into my bedroom, they would think I encouraged him. I just couldn't believe how stupid he was to do this. I can't believe him. I'm so angry with him. Who does he think I am? "Just go, you're unbelievably stupid! Just get out!"

He had to go back out the way he came. From the water pipes, he climbed down and onto the kitchen roof, then jumped to a shorter wall before finally jumping from the outdoor toilet. I was so angry with him for doing this. We didn't speak for a few weeks because I was very upset and hurt by it all.

He told me he loved me and we were going to get married. I fell for his stupid lies, so he entered the house again. I was so worried. What if my dad or my mum heard any noises and came into my bedroom? What would I do? I was not up for this at all.

I told him this but all he was saying was that he loved me and wanted us to get married. I felt the same about him. I gave in to his foolish, mad idea. I made sure the window was not locked and he came in that night. This was the night I lost my virginity. I felt it was not what I expected. It was painful and uncomfortable. It was the worst time in my life, because I really didn't want to do this but I went along with it because of how I felt about him. I didn't really want to do it. I knew it was wrong.

The next thing I heard, my mum's door open. I was so scared. He crawled under the table trying to make himself small. I felt so bad as I saw my mother standing in my doorway looking at us. My mum whispered, "Get out Daniel, go out how you came in," and he left. He glanced at me as I looked at him with disgust and disappointment. I thought, *yes, you did this to me. And you've gone and left me in a right mess and a lot of trouble.*

I was so ashamed and embarrassed. As I watched Mum's face, I saw the disappointment, disbelief, hurt and shame as she looked at me. It broke my heart. The tears rolled down my cheeks. I did what I never wanted to do, disappoint her. My mother looked at me with disgust and started slapping me on my arms and back. Then she left the room and went back into her bedroom. I was so ashamed. I didn't know how I would face my mother in the morning. I stayed in my room the next day as late as I could so I wouldn't have to face her. "Ronica, I'm going to work. I will talk to you when I get in tonight."

"Yes, Mum," I replied and I knew by the sound of her voice I was in trouble. All day, I was crying and hiding my tears. I felt disgusted with myself and felt I had betrayed my mum's trust. *What will she do? Will she hit me again?* I was frightened, feeling my stomach churning with anxiety and dreading going home that afternoon. I started thinking what could I do that would show her how sorry and ashamed I felt. I quickly did the cooking and left it on a low temperature. I went into my mum's bedroom and began sweeping the floor, changing the sheets and making the bed, and cleaning the dressing table. Making sure her bedroom was very tidy. After about 20 minutes, I checked the food, making sure the food was cooked. I made sure the kitchen and the dining room were spotless.

My father at this time would come in later, as he felt I was old enough to be left on my own until my mother got home, which was still 5.30pm to 6.00pm.

When Mum came in that evening, she wasn't very pleased and ignored me for some time during that evening. I just kept out of her way. As she went up into her bedroom and noticed it was tidy. She called me up and asked me, "Why did you do that, Ronnie? I am so upset and disappointed. I didn't bring you up to be so disrespectful. How can you do such a thing?"

"I'm so sorry, Mama, but he climbed through the window. I didn't tell him to do that."

"How long has this been going on? Tell me the truth?"

"It happened twice before and this was the third time. Mum, I'm so sorry. I will never do this again, Mama, I promise. I'm so sorry. Mama, we have been going out for two years, Mama. He would meet me from school, not every day. He would walk me to the back street behind the main road. Then I would come home, Mama. He climbed through the window one night and frightened me out of my sleep. I was very upset with him, because I didn't tell him to do this. Mama, I'm so sorry. I'm so sorry. I didn't really want this to happen. I'm so sorry. He talked me into allowing him in twice. Sorry Mama, I will not do this again, I promise."

"Did he wear any protection?"

"Yes, mama he did."

"Ronnie, I haven't brought you up this way and I'm very disappointed with you, because you could have done this better. It doesn't look good on you or me. Suppose your dad was the one that heard movement or voices in your room. It would have been trouble. He would have hit that boy with something, he would have hurt him badly and would have got into trouble. That boy could have lost his life."

I started crying because I knew it wasn't my fault but again, I did the wrong thing by not saying, "No."

After a few weeks I went to the park and saw him with a girl. I just couldn't believe my eyes. When I saw him with this girl, he looked at me and then looked away. I felt so hurt and so many feelings and thoughts went through my mind. How could he promise me we would be together and get married? I felt so small and embarrassed. Standing there feeling humiliated in front of all these people witnessing all of this, I just wanted the ground to swallow me up. I was overwhelmed. I turned and walked away as soon as I could. I couldn't stop the tears. I felt betrayed and the pain was excruciating.

Did he really feel anything for me? All the memories came flooding back, walking me home from school. He made me feel so special. I always felt a fluttering in my stomach, feeling he was mine alone. I felt nothing mattered as long as I had him. I felt warm and safe when he held me in his arms so tight and kissed me. I felt he really loved me and I really felt the same. The moments we had were so special. This was a shock to me. Even after seeing him with my own eyes, I still couldn't believe it.

Comforting Fruit & Nut

As I exited the park, I encountered Carlos; his manner was so kind and gentle, and I sensed a softer nature in him, even though he was older. He always said hello in passing. I have always known him as a friendly and happy natured person. Both our mothers spoke at length anywhere they saw each other, mostly in the market. I remember putting the shopping bags down as their conversation went on for some time.

He saw I was very upset that day and asked me, "Hi, are you ok?"

"No, I'm not," I replied. "I've just seen Daniel speaking to a girl. He saw me and ignored me completely. So, I've decided to go home."

I passed a shop just before, and bought the biggest chocolate, *Fruit & Nut*. I bought the chocolate to drown my sorrows, to make myself feel better. I can still remember the wonderful taste of that chocolate bar, sweet and creamy. I wasn't bothered about putting on weight nor feel any guilt about eating the whole bar. It was comforting and something only for me and no one could tell me I couldn't have it. I bought it with my spending money that I had saved up; it was my body; it was my time to enjoy and to feel whatever I felt. It was all about me at this moment.

Carlos was very kind and told me, "Don't worry, things will work out. Can I have some of your chocolate?" I gave him a piece; we said our goodbyes and went our separate ways. Not knowing that one day our paths would meet again.

After some weeks, I finished with Daniel and found out he had many girls after him. He had a part-time job delivering and selling pop with a driver. He became very popular with the girls. After seeing him in the park, avoiding my gaze, I believed he knew the mess he'd caused and was too ashamed to confront me or ever mention it again; the silence between us felt heavy with unspoken words and regret. Mum told me that his mother had also had a word with him and he felt so ashamed so probably it was easier for him to move on to someone else. It took me a long time to get over him.

5.
LEAVING SCHOOL

Shortly after this incident, I left school at 15 years. I was very concerned because I didn't acquire any CSE's at all. Because of this, my choices were very limited. My careers teacher told me I could only work in a factory. I was so upset and told her, "No, Miss, I will not be working in a factory." Seeing my mother's frantic workplace, cramped space and working constantly without breaks, I knew it wasn't for me. "I want to work in an office." This was the week before leaving school. I went around town to all the offices and asked, "Have you got any jobs at the moment? I'm willing to work." I remembered my mother telling me this was the way they got work when they came to England. I thought, *if it worked in my mother's time, why can't it work for me?* This particular time, it was pouring it down. Thank God I had an umbrella; this was a Friday. I had been walking in the rain for two hours. I approached another building with a buzzer, which I pressed and someone asked me, "How can I help you?"

I answered, "Have you got any job vacancies, please?"

"Just one minute, please. Can you come in, please?"

I replied," Yes, thank you."

I looked like a drowned rat. My hair was wet and my afro had shrunk to half its length; my black and white large, printed coat was drenched, and the umbrella was dripping with water. As I entered the door and walked up the stairs, I could feel I was soaked and heard the squelching noise of the water in my shoes. There was another door. I rang a bell and a man came to the door dressed smartly in his suit, which had black and green stripes in it. I remember his suit because green was my favourite colour.

He told me to come in. He looked at me from top to bottom and said, "Oh love, you're drenched. Can I help you?"

"Yes, sir, I hope you can. I'm looking for a job. Have you got any vacancies at all, sir?"

He looked at me, eyebrow raised and said, "Have you been walking in the rain looking for a job?"

"Yes, sir." I replied.

"For how long?"

"Since 10.00am, sir."

"It's 2pm now. Come into my office and sit down so we can talk. What's your name? How old are you?"

"I'm 15 sir."

"Ok." he said.

As he started writing my name, age, and other details, I felt so happy. I was just thanking God in my heart. "So, we have a junior clerk post vacant at the moment. We will train you and teach you what you need to know. How does that sound to you?"

"That sounds great, thank you, sir!"

"Can you start this Monday coming?"

"Yes, sir?"

"You will be paid £7.50pw. How does that sound to you?"

"That sounds very good, sir."

"Ok, we will see you at 9.00am on Monday."

"Thank you, thank you very much, sir. See you Monday." As I left the building, I couldn't wait to tell my careers teacher and Mama about my job. I prayed, "God, thank for helping me to get a job today." As I prayed, I felt the tears filling my eyes and rolling down my face. I felt the warmth and love from within. I was so happy and thankful to get this job.

My niece, who was very clever usually passed all her exams. I was glad for her. However, people in the family looked and thought, I wasn't academically good enough. I felt this was my chance to prove to myself, *I can do all things through Christ that strengthens me.*

Working and Studying

The first day at work. It was very daunting not knowing what to expect. *How will they be with me and will I be accepted? I'm the only black person in the entire building. How will they treat me? Will they like me? How will I learn everything I need to know?* All these things came into my mind. As I thought about these questions, I remembered what my mother told me, "Ronnie just try to do your best and your best will be good enough, be polite to everyone because this is the way forward, you are as good as anyone, God is always with you, just remember that and you will be ok." The memory of my mother's voice and her encouraging thoughts filled my head as I walked toward the building; this time, I wasn't seeking a job, I was already an employee. Thank you, God, for making this happen. Let everything go according to your will and plan. I rang the buzzer and gave my name; the door unlocked. As I walked upstairs, I couldn't feel my legs. I was very nervous and I could feel my heart pounding within my chest. *Oh God, please help me. I'm so scared. Please let everything go well for today. Please let them be nice to me.*

As I open the door, Mr James greeted me. "Good morning, Veronica, how are you today?"

"I'm ok Sir."

"Good. Now, I will introduce you to Sue, who will teach you all you need to know and how to deliver the post in the area. It usually takes around half an hour to 45minutes." Mr. James walked me to a different office and there was Sue. My first impression of Sue was good. She had shoulder length hair, which was blonde, very wispy at the ends, she appeared very nice with a friendly smile. She had a round shaped face with a broad smile. Medium size and dressed very casually with flat black shoes.

"Sue, meet Veronica. It's her first day here, and I'm hoping you can show her the ropes like you were shown. She needs to learn where to deliver the mail, file things, post letters, stamp envelopes, and whatever else her junior clerk job involves." Sue nodded. "Thanks, Sue, have a good day. If there is something you're not sure about, just ask Sue or if Sue's not available, you can ask me, is that ok, Veronica?"

"Yes, thanks very much, Mr James." As he left, I watched him in his grey smart suit. And thanked God that he had given me a boss that seemed nice and genuine.

It appeared to me that Sue was very conscious of her face, as she would always stroke her hair and guide it towards her face. As though she wasn't comfortable with her hair pulled back. She told me about her experiences in the company. "I have worked here for almost a year. The people are nice and friendly. There are a few people who are... bizarre. You will find out for yourself, I'm sure."

After watching Sue work for a while, I remarked, "I can see you're really good at your job, aren't you. How long did it take you to learn all the skills you have gained? You're excellent and quick at folding letters and using the stamp machine." I was also very impressed by the filing systems that were in place for clients and companies in the basement. I hadn't seen metal shelves fixed around the walls before, with each shelf in alphabetical order to identify all the clients and companies. Also, the boxes that were sealed with all the information for clients and companies that had been with this organisation for years.

Overwhelmed, I told Sue, "This is too much to remember. I'm sure I will get used to the system. As you said, I will get the hang of things eventually."

Working at this company allowed me to see the world in a different light. The office was very busy. Entering, I saw four large tables, each supporting three stacked trays. The workspace was a large room with three rows of tables and a central area partitioned off by glass for the telephonist and typist. Sue and I worked at a wide table dedicated to mail, with another office containing three more tables situated behind us. There was frosted glass, so you could just about see who was in this office. This was where Garry and Anne worked. This section dealt with complaints from all clients. There were also trays of letters, which had to be collected for the post.

One day I noticed there was a lot of playing going on. Garry was grabbing Anne, and they were laughing. I thought this was very weird and inappropriate. The behaviour was appalling. I turned to face the telephonist. The noises and movements they were making had been going on for some time, visible even through the frosted glass. Everyone else was busy attending to different cases and seemed not to notice.

One day I was collecting the post, I could hear Garry and Anne play fighting with each other. I continued working but still had an eye on their movements. I saw Garry grab Anne from the back and put his hands on each of her breasts. When they realised I saw them, they both sat still, like nothing ever happened. I turned towards the telephonist. I could see she was blushing as she was red as a beetroot. I said, "Why do they do that? Don't they realise we can see them?"

Her reply was, "It's been going on for so long that people don't take any notice of them. Let them get on with it."

"They both have partners, don't they? How can they do this to their partners?"

This went on each day, but despite this, they worked very hard and got the work done. Nevertheless, the behaviour was disgusting and disrespectful because Garry was married and Anne had a fiancé. I got the impression that it was a big laugh for them both and embarrassing for other colleagues. They never came out with us; they would be in the office every day, for the three and a half years I worked at this company.

When everyone went out for lunch, was an eye-opening experience for me. The amount they would drink shocked me.

They would ask, "what do you want to drink Veronica?"

"It's ok, I will get my own drink."

"No, what do you want to drink? Said Richard.

"I'll have an orange juice, please."

"What do you want with it?"

"Nothing, thanks."

Some of them would offer me another, as the drink I bought lasted me for an hour. "I can't believe you still have the same drink!"

"I don't really drink a lot of alcohol." Was my reply.

The amount of liquor they drank was unbelievable; yet they functioned at work, surprisingly.

The first job on a morning was to hand deliver all the mail to the companies that were close to the office. Around 4pm everyone had a tray on their desk labelled POST. The letters that were in these trays had to be gathered, stamped, and posted.

On the lengthy, large table at the back of the office, all the letters were folded and put in envelopes to be stamped by a machine. Sue trained me, and in time I understood how the system worked. I continued to be very vigilant, making sure everything I did was right. Sue made me feel comfortable by saying, "Don't worry, it takes time to memorise all that needs to be done each day, but you will get the hang of it."

After a few weeks I felt I had mastered the job. All the people who worked in the office were very nice but I soon found out not to be too friendly. My mother had warned me, "They can change in a second." I made sure I didn't tell them very much about my private life and stayed friendly and polite to everyone.

5.
SELF

I enrolled on a shorthand and typing course. I felt I had to continue educating myself. Going to college on Tuesdays and Thursdays was amazing. This allowed me to stay motivated and encouraged me to stay focused on moving forward towards my goal. I wanted to learn to type and shorthand. This would give me the skills to progress and push myself to achieve something more in life. I have always been ambitious but felt I couldn't achieve because of my spelling. I didn't know why but I wasn't going to settle for second best. I wanted to be someone who would help others like me to survive and be accountable for my own actions. To prove to that career's teacher and all the other people that thought I wasn't good enough. Success required hard work and qualifications. This was a new chapter and a new season, to see what the future holds for me. I knew without hard work I couldn't achieve and move forward without trying different things in life. Going to college also allowed to push myself to overcome my fear of not being good enough. I had to do this alone. This was my path of healing myself from past labels. This was the real reason I had to go to college. This was my escape from within myself. Hoping, aspiring to be better, to be someone that I could be proud of.

As I was now working, my parents allowed me to go out on Saturdays with my friends. Before I went out, I had to get up early to wash everyone's clothes by hand. I washed the white clothes first, ensuring they were spotless before washing the coloured items.

Meeting - Carlos again

Bonfire Night was exciting in those days. Everyone would meet at a particular place each year. Arriving at this place, I saw people getting too excited and throwing bangers at one another. Carlos saw me and we started talking. He was the guy who asked me for some chocolate over a year ago. I knew his mother and he knew my mum and dad as well. I knew he lived at home with his mum.

Carlos asked, "Do you want to come to my house until it calms down a bit?"

"Ok." I said.

When we got into his house, he took me to this room and turned on the light, then I realised it was his bedroom. He pointed at the bed and said, "You can sit there." I suddenly thought differently about him; I was wary. I was determined that I would do nothing with him. Carlos sat next to me and started talking. After a while, he said, "You look terrified; I'm not going to hurt you."

I said, "I know but I would like to go now."

Carlos said, "OK." and kissed me. I was eased back onto the bed. I felt safe with him, but I knew it would only be a kiss.

As we lay on the bed looking at each other, he said, "I will not hurt you." His eyes were light brown. He spoke quietly and appeared kind and sincere. I really felt very different with Carlos, so I reminded myself to play it cool. I knew this was the first time, and this thought came in my head, *Don't give yourself away too easily, because It's not good.* I decided I would not do anything that would make me feel cheap. He knew I wasn't up to this and said, "Ok, are you ready to go?"

"Yes, I am actually." I blurted out. He was a gentleman; he made me feel safe. Again, I noticed his gorgeous light brown eyes, straight nose, and handsome face and delicious scent. He also had a small, shaped beard. He was so handsome.

Carlos walked me home that evening. He was warm and good-humoured, sharing funny stories that had me laughing along the way. I genuinely enjoyed his company. When we reached the bottom of my street, Carlos offered, "I can walk you right to your door to make sure you get in safely."

"It's ok," I said, "because my mum will be looking out of the window and I don't want her to see you walk me home?"

"Alright, you take care of yourself. We will see each other soon." Carlos kissed me on my cheek and I walked up the street to my house. Our paths didn't cross again for many years.

I went grocery shopping early Saturday, about a seven-mile round trip, for the weekend's food. When I got back, I had to wash the whites and hang them on the washing line in the back garden. Then wash the coloured clothes (we didn't have a washing machine or a Hoover). Whilst the coloured clothes were soaking, I would sweep from the top of the house to the bottom with a brush and hand shovel. After doing all my chores, I would lie down for an hour before getting ready to go out at 7.30pm.

The town would buzz with people of all nationalities. Going to the planned venue was exciting. We danced around our handbags, drank in moderation and if we were asked for a dance, that was good too. We had fun.

I met Stephen, who preferred to be called Steve. He was very handsome and was in the territorial army part time. When he came up to me and asked me for a dance. I felt like a little girl. He was so charming and polite. I really liked what I saw. He was a bit taller than me; he had perfect teeth, which was good. I always look after my teeth, as I love to smile. The words "All that glitters is not gold," spoken by my mother, echoed in my ears; only later did I learn it was a quote from William Shakespeare.

Steve was very polite and asked me if he could take me out next week Saturday. The answer was "Yes, ok."

Once all of us girls were ready to go, we would decide on the arrangements for who would accompany whom at each bus stop to catch our late busses. One of my friends was going with me as arranged. We looked at each other as Steve approached. He walked up to the bus stop and asked, "Can I come for you next week? Where do you live?"

I was hesitant to give him my address. "Oh, I can meet you in town next week, is that ok?"

"Yes, of course. What time is good for you?"

"Around 7.30pm at Lewis'?"

"That's great! Ok, that's fine." He held my hand and said, "See you next week at Lewis's."

My friend said, "He seems nice. Do you like him?"

"He's really good looking; he looked great in his uniform."

All I could think about was his face.

"Yes, he is handsome, isn't he?"

"I couldn't believe, when he came over to me and spoke to me. Well, I do like him, but like my mum always says, 'All that glitters is not gold!' So, I'll have to see what he is like." (My mother was a first-class student, very knowledgeable, and good with words).

The next week I met in town at Lewis's, as promised. He was in his uniform again. I asked him, "What do you do in the territorial army and how does it work, being part time?"

"We are taught how to use a gun; we have to be trained enough so we can defend ourselves in case there is any trouble." I really enjoyed talking to him. He was so ambitious and had a direction. He knew what his goals were and knew what he wanted in life. I found him very attractive and knowledgeable. We went for a drink, and then he asked me what I wanted to do. I wanted to talk to him all night, but I knew I couldn't, so we went to a club. We danced all night, and he insisted he would make sure I got home by taxi. I agreed. Because I really liked his ambitious attitude. He kissed me goodnight before we got to the bottom of my street. I didn't want my mum to see us. We arranged another date for the next week Saturday.

We continued to meet and eventually decided to have a relationship. He asked what I did during the week, and if we could meet up during the week? "Well, I go to college twice a week," I told him.

"What are you studying?"

"I'm studying shorthand and typing because I work in an office and I want to go up the ladder. I have been there for over one year now."

"Do you like it?"

"Yes, I do. I enjoy the work and the people are very nice."

Steve was from Jamaica. He came over to the UK when he and his brother were very young. He was 5ft 7ins. His complexion was fair, his face oval, his eyes dark brown, his teeth attractive, and his hair short. He had a beautiful smile, and a laugh that was contagious. He came across as a very joyful and polite person. He was very giving and kind. He would help anyone who needed help. He was always gentle and kind to me.

I didn't introduce him to my parents, as I used to hear a lot of negative statements about other people from different countries.

One evening we went to his friend's house, who was also in the part-time territorial army. I saw a gun and startled, I said, "Steve, there's a gun there, wow is it real?"

Yes, it's real. Do you want to know how it works?"

"I don't really know. It looks frightening." He started pointing the gun straight ahead and guided me to look through the barrel of the gun.

It was time for me to go so he took the gun from me and pointed it towards the floor, then he pulled the trigger, and I started screaming, "Oh my GOD! My foot!" I realised he had shot me in my knee.

He shouted," What's wrong Ver? What's wrong Ver?"

"I think you shout me in my knee!"

Devastated, he apologised, helped me down the stairs, and took me to the hospital. I told him to leave and I would tell them what happened. He really didn't want me to do this on my own. I reassured him that I knew he didn't do this on purpose.

Hospital staff eventually demanded to know if the incident was intentional and where it occurred. I vouched it was accidental. After they injected the painkiller into my knee, they tried to take the pellet out with a pair of scissors, using them as a magnet. I could still feel the pain. It was excruciating. In the end, I had to have an operation to get the pellet out of my knee.

The police went to the house to let my parents know what had happened. I was dreading going home because I knew what my father was like. I had to be assisted by crutches and taken back home in an ambulance. When I arrived, all the lights were on. I thought I'm in big trouble now. When my father saw me with crutches, he said to me, "It's your coffin should be coming in the door tonight. You stupid girl." I was horrified, but expected nothing better from my father.

My mother said, "Ronnie, you could have lost your leg! What happened, Ronnie? Come, I'm so pleased to know you're ok." I cried and told my mum what really happened. She was so happy I was ok and I could still use my foot. I was told not to go back out with him again. He felt really upset that it had happened. We didn't see each other for a while.

My father always said unless someone was from West Indies (the Caribbean) they would mistreat you. I didn't believe this, as my father was West Indian and was not an angel. I witnessed him beating and cursing my mother on numerous occasions. I recall ducking as my mother threw the hot teapot at my father. She gave as much as she got. This is why I always just freeze when I see anyone fighting.

I then started going to Steve's house after he took me to meet his mother, who was very nice. She was short, spoke softly and always greeted me well. We became very close and she would remind Steve to look after me because, "She's a nice girl."

After a few weeks I told my mum that I was still going out with Steve. One day, he told me that this girl was always chasing him and something happened. "What happened?" I asked him.

"She says she is pregnant."

I was devastated and disappointed that he would two-time me. "I thought you were in love with me? I wouldn't go with anyone else whilst I'm going out with someone. Well,, marry her and she should have the baby. It's the right thing to do."

I was heartbroken because I really loved him. So, this was how we finished.

Later on, he married her. A few years later she approached me, telling me that every time they had an argument, he would blame her for breaking up with me. I told her he shouldn't do that because everyone has to take responsibly for what they do in their life. Some years later, I saw him in the park at Carnival time. He looked well; he was divorced. He had left the army years ago. His mum had died. "Your mum was a lovely person." I spoke. He still looked well after all these years. I was happy to see him.

6.
First Marriage

Years went by, and I gained my qualification in typing and shorthand. I got promoted. I became a junior telephonist/ copy typist. I stayed at my first job for three and a half years. I felt I needed more experience at other offices. So, I did temporary work. This allowed me to have more experience of other people's styles of working and allowed me to work in different companies. I enjoyed it as it allowed me to gain more experience and knowledge within other companies.

Working in different offices allowed me to expand my mindset. My attitude changed, which allowed me to look at individuals as equals. Human beings do the best we can with the knowledge we have acquired. I was working one day and looked out of the window. To my surprise, I looked out and this young man looked up. Our eyes met but that was it. After some time, I noticed him when I went out one night. He said hello and I said hello.

After that, we noticed each other and we would smile and have small talk. "How are you?"

"I'm ok thanks."

"How are you?"

"I'm ok thanks."

Until one day he asked me out. His name was Gary. We planned to meet but something went wrong for me that evening. I ended up arriving an hour late. I was very surprised that he was still there. I apologised. "I thought you weren't coming." He spoke.

"I'm so sorry. I got held up and I couldn't get here any quicker. Sorry about that." I remember wearing a green dress and he always commented on it, making me feel a bit embarrassed about the style. I found out later; he criticised a lot.

We dated for some time. I liked him. At home one evening, to my surprise, the bell rang. Gary and another person arrived at the door selling insurance. He told me he had another job part-time. I told my mum someone was at the door. She welcomed them into the house. My father started asking Gary questions, "Who are your mother and father? Where do you live?" As he told him who his mum was, my father said, "Oh! I know your mother!" and called her by a name (with a big grin on his face).

I looked at my mother and she said, "Yes, I know your mum." and said nothing more.

After Gary and the person with him had finished explaining the business to my parents. I saw them to the door. Gary and I said goodbye at the door and agreed to meet as planned, which was the coming Saturday at 7.30 in town. This was the first time I had ever heard my dad say a good word about anyone. I felt ok; he liked Gary, and that was good for me.

I told my mum after some time that we were going out with each other. When she told my father, for some unknown reason, he was ok with it. Mum said to me one day, "Ronnie, you have to bring him to the house to meet your dad and me."

"Ok Mum."

About two weeks after the conversation with my Mum, I invited Gary to come and meet my parents. Gary was very unsettled, not knowing what my father would say. I was unsettled myself. When he arrived at the house, I was jittery. This was the first boy I had ever introduced to my parents. I was nervous and wondered what my dad would say to him. The bell rang, and in he came. I could tell he was petrified and whispered, "Are you ok?"

"Yes, I am. Are you?"

"To be honest, I'm a bit nervous." I confessed.

I went into the dining room first, then Gary followed. "Good afternoon, Mr. and Mrs. Edwards. How are you today?" I could hear the nerves in his voice as he cleared his throat. It felt like we're going into the lion's den and we didn't know what was going to happen. The room felt tense and was silent. Dad had turned off the tv, he meant business.

"I understand you like my daughter?"

"Yes, I do, Mr. Edwards."

"Well, I'm wanting to talk to you because I want you to know I have worked hard to bring her up. If you're going to go out with her, I don't want you to ill-treat her, because I will not be happy. That's all I want to tell you face to face." My dad stated.

My mum said, "Well, you are both young and if you both like each other, you must look after each other. But if you know you both are not suited, then you don't have to stay and hurt each other, either. You both are young, and there is someone for everyone." I was shocked because I didn't know what to expect from both of my parents. I felt it went very well.

We went out every weekend. Usually, we would go to parties around where he lived. I lived about three miles from his house. I had been going out with him for one and a half years when we planned to have a baby. Looking back on this decision, we loved each other but were very immature at this time. Sometimes I blame the movies I watched, when everything ended up good in the end, even though I've never regretted having my daughter. I was 19 years of age when I gave birth to her. Mother thought I was using the contraceptive pill and was very disappointed to find out I was pregnant.

This was the same year my Mum was going to the West Indies. My father was very upset I got pregnant and mistreated me throughout my pregnancy. He would say, "Move out of the way, and let me pass". He was furious even to see me. He couldn't stand it. I stayed out of his way as I felt he would hit me. My Mum had already booked her fight to go to the West Indies just before I got pregnant. He said to my mother, "When you leave, and you're flying in that airplane, she will be on the street. I'm going to throw her out of my house."

I was frightened that night when my mother left. Gary stayed, without my Dad knowing, in case my he forced his way into the room to throw me out. That night I didn't sleep because I was so frightened for myself and the life of my daughter.

I knew I had to leave home. My cousin (out of respect, I call her sister Loretta) told me to come and stay with her for a while.

That night was long and very worrying, as I thought of my poor Mother heart broken, not knowing what would happen to me tonight. Very early that morning, I had all my bags packed and left.

I was at my cousin's flat with her three children and her. I felt very humbled and thankful and felt her kindness towards me and a crying baby. If baby Crystal felt the sunlight on her, she would cry. My baby cried at anything at all. She stayed most of the time on the dining table so we could make sure she was ok. She was a crier and it was hard as she was my first child, at 19 years of age.

My cousin showed me how to deal with my crying baby and helped me to look after her, which I was so grateful for. While my mother was in the West Indies visiting her sisters and family that she hadn't seen for several years, I missed her so much. I used to wonder how my mum was managing so far away from the baby and me. I made sure I contributed to the home and helped to tidy and treat my sister's home like I would my own. Gary came to see his daughter and me at the house but didn't stay over. After about six months, a bedsit two doors away from my sister's house became available. I decided to live there.

A friend of my mother told me I should marry Gary, because I have a child from him and he may leave me and get someone else and marry them. The very thought of this was worrying. I told Gary how I felt about getting married.

We both decided we wanted to get married. We had a child now and wanted to be a family. We didn't have the money to have a big wedding so we married at the register office. One of our friends did it and it made sense. I told my mum when she came back from her holidays. I knew my mum was disappointed but I didn't want to put my mum in a position of paying for this wedding. I told my mum she didn't have to come. We had two friends who would be our witnesses. It would be great if she came after work.

We bought a sponge cake and some juice, so when Mum came, she had a slice of cake and a drink. When Mum came to the bedsit, I saw she was not too happy but she said nothing. (I didn't know how painful it was for my mother for me to get married under these circumstances.) She was not used to this kind of thinking and attitude and found it very embarrassing and hurtful that her last daughter married in this way.

Later, as I got older, I realised how sensitive that must have been for my mother. Mum recounted in our later conversation; I'd told her about my marriage and asked her not to visit. "That really hurt me. I cried all the way home that evening when you offered me a slice of sponge cake and fruit juice." Hearing it from my mum it would have been excruciating to hear. Especially as I'm the youngest of five siblings.

The bedsit was so small. We had to eat, sleep, and cook in the same room. With a baby, it was very difficult. It got on top of us and, to make it worse, Gary got vertigo. He became very irritable, picking at every little thing. I got sick of him shouting at me and told him, "I will not stand for this aggressive behaviour." To my horror and surprise, he started hitting me. I said, "Why are you raising your hand to me? I'm not having it!" He started hitting me regularly. I didn't stand for it so I hit him back. It was getting out of control; I used to go to church regularly. Then, one Sunday when I went to church, I asked the vicar to speak to him. He came and told us that living in a bedsit, which was not healthy. I didn't want to tell my mum about this because I knew if my dad found out, he would come and it would get nasty.

I then tried to get a flat by going to the council and explaining our living conditions.

As we had our first baby, we were offered a flat that was very suitable and we took it. Things were better but he still thought he had the right to bully me. I was determined that he would not bully or hit me and me not hit back. He returned to a job he no longer wanted, having been off sick for some time, despite suffering from vertigo. I was working in an office and a childminder was recommended to me. She looked after baby Crystal; she was clean and looked settled when I collected her. In those days there were no such things as disposable nappies and if there were, I couldn't afford them. So, each evening demanded a soaking and washing of soiled nappies.

I added softener to keep them soft and smelling fresh and I dried them in front of the fire, ready to be used again the day after. As baby Crystal was a crier, I was always praying that she wouldn't get on this woman's nerves, so she would take care of her. I always checked baby Crystal for anything unusual. I had to work but I was paying for a service and expected my baby to be treated well.

The childminder complained to my mother's friend about my baby's constant crying. "I'm going home now because I left her on her own in the cot while I come to town for something. See you soon." When this lady heard whose child it was, she told mum and mum told me. I heard about this news on Tuesday by Thursday I had a new job at the cinema, I had to work on the Thursday and Friday evening, I didn't care, I was worried about my baby girl and I had to get her out of this woman's place quickly. So, I prayed, "Oh Heavenly Father, please make a way where there is no way. Oh, Lord, just provide a way out for us and make the way clear so we can be victorious in this situation, Amen."

I told my employer on the Wednesday morning that I had to leave as this woman is leaving my 6-month-old baby in the house on her own. I told them I would have to leave at the end of the week. They waived my notice period because of the emergency. It was so good of the manager to agree to this; I had worked there for two years. I had to leave my office job on Friday and get a job for the next week, working in the evenings. I told Gary he had to collect and look after baby Crystal until I got back. I had to go into town to look for suitable work starting the next week. I went to all the cinemas to ask if they had any jobs. I got a job the same evening after walking for hours at the ABC cinema as an usherette. I had to work on Thursday and Friday evenings from 5.30pm until 10.30pm to secure this job at the cinema. I knew I had to try to get as much sleep as possible tonight and tomorrow. So, Gary had to collect baby Crystal from the childminder on the Thursday and I would collect her on the Friday.

As she opened the door, I said," Hello, how are you doing?" I went into the house as usual. After she'd gathered all the nappies together and told me how Crystal had been all day, I said, "Thanks for looking after Crystal. I will not be bringing her back. I will look after her from now on." I then left her shocked and wondering what had happened. I saw her around the area but I didn't speak to her and she would turn her head when she saw me. It didn't bother me at all.

I started my job at the cinema the same week. I continued working there for 13 years. I'd work in the evening from 5.30pm to 10.30pm from Monday to Friday. Gary would look after baby Crystal in the evenings. He continued working for a while, then told me he was not working for the white man anymore. So, in the days he would go out to the pub and looked after baby Crystal while I worked. He complained of illness but played cards and dominoes at the pub, yet he refused to work.

Our neighbour who lived downstairs had separated from her partner. They were a European couple. I tried to speak and be friendly but I noticed she was not forthcoming with wanting to speak. Her partner was more friendly and would say hello as our paths crossed going into the building. They lived downstairs and we lived upstairs. I knew that they would have heard when we had any arguments, as we could hear them when they had any arguments too. Days went by and I noticed I didn't see her partner. I saw the child, as she would allow the child to go into the garden with a tee shirt, her knickers, and no shoes on her feet. This had been going on for years. Winter or summer didn't matter. I didn't agree with this kind of treatment of children.

Returning home from work one evening, I found Gary in the bedroom watching TV, with baby Crystal in his arms, and his ex-girlfriend sitting on the bed next to him. I felt really upset and wanted to throw her out, but I'm not like that. It felt so wrong.

She said "Hello."

I said, "Hi,"

After a few minutes, she said, "I'm going now."

I took baby Crystal from him, and he walked her out. I made sure I was at the top of the stairs, looking down. When he came back up the stairs, I asked, "Why was she in my bedroom?"

"Well, it's cold in the living room and I would have to take baby Crystal into the cold room." He replied.

"If you came home and met me in the bedroom with one of my exes, how would you like it?" I enquired.

"Well, we weren't doing anything, baby Crystal was here," as he looked at me in amazement.

I replied, "Who do you take me for?" It made little sense to me. I thought if he wanted to, he could put baby Crystal in her cot and do anything, and he knew what time I came in the house.

From this day I didn't trust him. Much later on, another incident came up when he told me something had happened and he can't keep it from me any longer. He had sex with the neighbour downstairs. I was devastated. We almost finished for this one. I asked him, "How did it happen?"

"Well, she started speaking to me one day as I was going out."

"Where did it happen?"

"She rang the bell another day and she started talking about why she and her partner finished? Because he was not happy with their relationship."

"When did it happen? I asked.

"She rang the bell again and I invited her up. I took her into the front room, then one thing led to another."

After I heard the whole story, I was so angry I didn't even want to look at him. I thought you disrespected me. "Why did you invite her into our home? Did you two plan this? Why didn't you go downstairs to her place? Has this been happening for a while?"

"No," he said, with tears in his eyes, "I'm really sorry. It will not happen again, I promise."

"Do you feel I'm a pushover, to put up with nonsense like this?" I looked at him in disgust.

"No, I don't think you're a pushover at all." as he looked at me pitifully.

"You're having a laugh. Is that why you invited your ex-girlfriend into our home, too?" I looked at him, thinking I've had enough of him.

"Now that's not true. Nothing happened with her; she just passed by because she hadn't seen me for a long time. I'm telling you the truth."

I looked at him and thought, *he really is taking me for a fool*. "Alright then. So, when I see my ex-boyfriends and they want to see me, I'll tell them they can visit. Ok?"

By then I'd had enough of his stupid explanations and nonsense. Now I knew what I was dealing with and who this person was. I lost all respect for him that day and decided I would do things differently for me and my child, because I didn't trust him anymore. I was so fed up with this fool and his weak, lazy attitude.

I felt I had to think of my child and our future. Shortly after this incident, I found out I was pregnant with my second child. I wanted my child but was very unsure of Gary. I had changed toward him and he sensed it. He would ask me, "What's wrong, Veronica?" He continued to try. I was very quiet and withdrawn. I spoke if I had to. I became very unhappy and sick of his adulterous ways. I could feel the tension between us but I felt he had done the dirty on me. Why should I feel sorry for him? I wanted him to think about his actions and get back to me.

One day we were in the kitchen and he came up to me and started invading my space. He came close to my face and asked me, "What's wrong with you? Why are you not speaking?"

"I'm ok, I'm fine, I just have a lot on my mind." I responded. To my surprise, he held me tight. I told him to let me go. I tried to wriggle out of his grip. "Why are you doing this? You know I'm still upset with you." He squeezed me harder. "Can you leave me alone, please?" I protested. He loosened his grip for a moment and as I walked away, he grabbed me and slapped me in the face. I was so shocked, I retaliated by slapping him back in his face, saying, "Don't you ever hit me in my face or put your hand on me ever!" He started hitting me again, so I grabbed his hand and bit his small finger hard, which stopped him from hitting me.

"I'm going to show this to my mother!" he screamed pathetically.

"You can tell whoever you want! You shouldn't be hitting me at all, especially as I am pregnant. I'm no one's punching bag!"

Then he got his coat and went out. He came back later and didn't speak. I was glad. I didn't want to hear anything about his finger. I'm not allowing anyone to hit me. He started doing this when we lived in the bedsit and he promised he wouldn't do it again. I'd seen my father hitting my mum for years, and I would not stand for anyone hitting me.

When I eventually visited his mother's house, she asked me, "You nearly bit off his small finger."

"Well, he shouldn't hit me at all, and I'm pregnant. I'm not having it." I got the impression that in his mother's eyes, Gary was always right. No matter what he did to me. No matter what I did, it wouldn't be good enough. I sensed her disbelief. She underestimated me, and again, I was not good enough.

During this time, within the marriage, my mother was my stronghold. She knew everything that was going on in this relationship. I felt my mother was my rock, apart from God, whom I completely trusted. When I told my Mum I was pregnant, she said, "Children are blessing, Ron, and they will look after you. Just make sure you look after them." My mum was very supportive throughout this journey. She was a great Mum who only wanted the best for everyone, but she didn't like people taking advantage of others. Gary was still not being responsible for his children or himself. He felt that by not working, the world and the government owed him something. I continued working at the cinema and again started progressing from an usherette to working as a cashier; working in the foyer, selling the tickets and being in charge of the ice cream room where all the ice cream was stored. Sometimes, I would sell drinks at the bar.

Because I sold the most magazines in the company from the foyer, I won an amazing all expenses paid weekend getaway for two. This experience was the first time for both me and Gary in a 4-star hotel. In the lobby were the most amazing light fixtures. It was overwhelming walking through this luxurious lobby. As I approached the desk, I told the receptionist my name. She called a member of staff, who showed us to our room. Entering the room, we could see that the room was also outstanding. It had a double bed, which had wonderful bedding and pillows organised in a special way. The curtains matched the bed throw. Large TV on the wall with a remote control. Sidelights on either side of the bed with a special design in a shiny gold colour. The bathroom had a large walk-in shower, a large face basin with golden taps, with a toilet to match. There were white mats on the floor and large and small towels folded on a small table, with shower gel, face, and body creams. The large bath towels were draped over the radiators.

Looking out of the window was delightful, with a lot of greenery and different coloured flowers. An extended covered area for sitting outside in case it rained. I felt rather hungry and realised it was time for lunch. "Let's get some lunch."

"Yes, I'm hungry too."

"Let's go. Where is the key?"

"It's here on the bed."

"Ok, let's go." We headed down to the foyer. Taking the lift was quick and it led to the dining area. As we entered, a member of staff greeted us and took us to our table. As we sat down, I looked around and my eyes caught this woman who was looking at us. I took my eyes off her and began looking at the menu. Gary also brought to my attention the fact that people were staring at us. I continued looking at the menu but took small glances at the few people watching us. "Yes, we are being stared at." I said to Gary. I then realised that they may not have seen a black couple in this facility before.

I looked at one of the staff members and smiled and nodded my head. She came over immediately and asked, "Are you ready to order, madam?"

"Yes, we are." We ordered our meal and the waitress left to get our order ready. Gary was still watching and noticing how many people were watching us. "Just don't worry about them. We are here and entitled to be here like anyone else. Let's just block them out and enjoy this moment."

"Yes, I agree." Gary said.

We were served all we had ordered. We said little to each other; we were hungry and concentrated on how lovely the lunch was. "That was absolutely delicious. What did you think?" Gary said.

"I really enjoyed that."

"Yes, it was very nice. Do you want anything else, a cup of tea or a cold drink?"

"Yes, are you having anything else?"

"Yes, I think a cup of tea would be good."

"Ok, I will have a drink. Do you want to order this time?" I asked Gary.

"Ok, I will."

Gary ordered. I noticed we were still getting slight stares, but I just smiled and ignored them and tried not to let them spoil anything out of this experience. I have had to deal with this all my life. It will not spoil my peace or affect this time that I so deserve and worked so hard to achieve. After our drinks, we looked around the hotel to see what more it offered.

We were so full after lunch, so we went to our comfortable room with fantastic views of London to rest. I was very relaxed and taking everything in. I wanted to know Gary's thoughts. "What do you think about all of this?"

"It's good," he said.

"Well, I thank God for this opportunity to experience this beautiful place and this moment."

"Yes, it's really good." I felt Gary enjoyed the experience but really didn't want to praise it too much, as I was the one that caused this to happen.

After a while, I awoke to see Gary watching the TV. "How long have you been up?"

"Not too long. I left you to enjoy your sleep."

"Oh, that's nice of you. I really needed the rest. I could feel the baby moving and probably enjoying the food too." Gary smiled and continued watching the TV. "We have to get dressed for dinner soon, we're also meeting Mark downstairs in the foyer."

"Do you know Mark?"

"No, I don't. We will meet him for the first time, according to the letter, in the lobby." Soon after, we began to shower and get dressed. We were going to meet Mark, who would tell us about the next day's arrangements.

As we made our way down to the lobby, we saw a man coming over to us. He greeted me, "Hi Veronica, I'm Mark." He held his hand out towards Gary and asked, "Hi, what is your name?"

"My name is Gary."

"Pleased to meet you both. Have you both enjoyed yourselves so far, Veronica?"

"Yes, so far, the hotel is great. Everyone is so helpful. Our lunch was just wonderful."

"Where do you live?" I asked Mark.

"I Live in London but I have visited your hometown a lot as I have family up there."

"Whereabouts?" I asked.

"North Yorkshire."

"Ok."

Mark went on to explain our itinerary. "You will be picked up at 5pm tomorrow evening. The show starts at 6pm, which gives you time to be seated, have a drink and observe the view. You will have a meal and drinks, which are also included. Is there anything you would like to ask me before I leave you both to have your evening meal?"

"Thanks very much for coming Mark, to enlighten us about the plan."

"You will be picked up, taken to see the show and the meal provided for you."

"So, we will see you tomorrow, here in the foyer, and look forward to seeing the show, too."

"Ok, I will see you both tomorrow. Have a great evening."

"I'm sure we will, and thanks again, bye." I watched Mark as he left. "He seems nice, doesn't he?"

"Yes, he does,"

"I'm really looking forward to the show tomorrow evening. Are you looking forward to the show,"

"Yes, I am actually."

I felt I had to always raise the point to see if he was enjoying himself. I now thought I'm not going to mention anything again and let him tell me what he felt about the experience.

My thoughts of the experience. Breakfast, lunch, and dinner were all provided as part of the package. The next day we were attending a show. Transport, meals, and drinks included, I had two tickets, with train tickets for two to travel. I took Gary and me. We went to see a show in London; we were given free meals, and the hotel was spectacular with rooms that were of a high standard. The experience was unlike anything Gary or I had ever encountered, leaving him quite overwhelmed. This caused me to continue to reach for the stars. My thoughts of the hotel, entering the lobby, the reception area. It was a first for both of us, a wonderful and eye-opening experience that offered a glimpse into another world.

This was the life. This made me realise that if I pray and work hard, I could have this life for me and my children. I felt Gary was overwhelmed but didn't want to show how he really felt because he didn't want me to get any credit for anything, or for me to feel good about myself, or to acknowledge me by saying you did really well to win this break for us. To say I made this happen.

After experiencing such a wonderful weekend, Gary took nothing from it at all. He went back to his miserable self. As I reached eight months, I was entitled to get my maternity benefit. During this time, Gary was working and couldn't have been at the birth anyway, as I had a Caesarean section. He came straight from work to see both of us.

Crystal had a very dark complexion but Marsha, my new baby, was very fair. Marsha and I had to spend 10 days in the hospital. My relationship with Gary wasn't great at this time but I was trying to make the most of it. I really wanted to move from the flat. We had two children now. I felt I should have a house so the children could have a back garden to play in. I mentioned it to Gary but he was so detached from moving forward it was unreal. He wasn't the man I knew; he had changed and was very negative and detached from reality. I had planned to return to work shortly after giving birth, but I had to delay going back to work too early because I needed to fully recover from the C-section. Also, I was unsure about Gary's ability to cope with looking after a newborn and a 3-year-old by himself. Would he be able to cope?

Eventually, I returned to work. I had to make sure that everything was ready before I left for work. He would start moaning and I just wanted to know the girls were ok.

I made sure dinner was always made and the girls were in clean nappies and had eaten before I left the house. Gary returned from work at 5.30pm and I had to leave as soon as he got in and returned at 11.15pm from work.

He began to chip away at the relationship. I realised he felt he was better than me. He felt very special, as though he had been put on a pedestal. I could feel the pressure of working and carrying him, the children, and myself. Everyone saw me working but saw him in the pub or sitting at home being lazy. This is when things crumbled. The marriage was in trouble and I didn't know what would happen if I had another child; I was struggling to cope with Crystal and Marsha. Then, just two months after having baby Marsha, I became pregnant again. He told me I had to get an abortion because he didn't want to feel embarrassed with two babies born so close together. I was very upset because I didn't believe in having abortions. It was against everything that God says and stands for. I knew it would be extremely difficult for me as Gary wasn't working. I felt so bad and felt I didn't have a choice; this would have been my BOY but how would I cope. I went through with the abortion. I felt so defeated and ashamed of what I had to do. I cried for weeks and months because I had killed my child. I always think about this and cry because it was not right and what he told me wasn't fair. I was married to this man; he should have put his child first, and I shouldn't have accepted his foolish, weak excuse for not being responsible for our actions. This baby deserved to live. This child was a gift and a human being. How could I go with this shallow decision? This was the turning point for me and this inconsiderate man. Now I lost all respect, and the deep love I had for him died with this child.

I knew things would never be the same again. I disliked him every time I looked at him; I would remember the words he said about our child. I felt he thought everyone was beneath him. The thought of people seeing me pregnant and baby Marsha not walking yet was unsettling to him. What a lame excuse.

7.
DANGEROUS TIMES

1975 to 1980 was a terrifying time for every woman, because the Yorkshire Ripper was going around killing women in the area. Travelling home was very frightening. Getting off the bus and being very vigilant and rushing as quickly as I could each night was the worst time of my entire life. Thanking God every night that I reached home safely to my girls. One girl who was killed by him was related to the family that lived next door. It was so terrifying and tragic. She was only very young, about 16 years old.

It was very stressful and dangerous coming home from work. I used to pray and run and walk, looking around frequently, making sure no one was behind me. The area saw women attacked and killed. This was the worst time for every woman in the area. No one was safe.

At this time, Gary was not feeling well and was now unemployed again. I had to continue because I knew where I wanted to be. Things were hard and difficult but this is when I depended on God to see me through. My mother was my rock and someone who was always there for me. Sometimes my mum would look at me and know I needed help and she would give me that help to continue my journey. This is why my mother came first as she became older. I didn't hesitate to look after her. I made sure she was looked after and wanted for nothing.

The bus I had to get to work was close to home and stopped outside the cinema, which was great. I went back to the council to enquire about a house. One day I walked around where I would like to live and this house strikingly stood out. The vacant house resembled a private residence, not council property. After contacting the office, I really prayed for this house because there was something about it I fell in love with. To my surprise, the council had just bought it and it needed some work done on it. I requested the house.

After speaking to the manager and telling him I had two children and the flat was too small for us now, and it would be great if the children could have a quiet backstreet to play out. At the flat, the door and the garden faced a busy main road and the children couldn't play in the garden. The answer came back, "Yes, but after the work has been done." It would take about six weeks.

I said, "Yes, I accept." I didn't even wait for Gary to see it. I told him I saw this house and I fell in love with it. It's not too far from where we lived. It was just across the road and a few streets down. It had a small lavender tree, which looked lovely. I really felt good about it. *Thank you, Father; you have done it again.*

I took Gary to see the house. "What you think?" I asked.

"Oh, it's ok, there is a lot of work to be done before we move in."

"I know but I think we can do one room at a time when we get in? What do you think?"

"Yes, I guess so. How much is it a week?"

"I can't remember, but it's not a lot more than we're paying now."

"Well, the rooms are not bad but we have to see if they will do something with the ceilings."

"I know it looks like the ceilings have been deliberately damaged."

"I thought that too. It looks like someone has taken a sweeping brush or a mop stick and pushed it into the ceiling tiles."

"It's the same damage in every room."

We had a look outside the house at the back. "The backstreet looks very clean."

"Yes, it looks ok and good for the children to play out."

"Yes, It's ok." I felt Gary had to be more convinced that the repairs had to be sorted, because I knew he was not wanting to do any decorating. I made sure when I went into the council office that I reported the damage and asked about the repairs. I was told that we could move in within four weeks and that the repairs would have been done by then. I was very excited.

For the next few weeks, I sorted out clothes we didn't want or were too small for the children and started packing things up. Gary wasn't enthusiastic about the move. I just continued to pack and stay focused on moving in four weeks. We moved and got into the house. Much decorating was still needed. I knew the council wouldn't decorate all the rooms. It was in our interest to do this.

After a few weeks, I started asking Gary when we'd start decorating. I was told that he was not feeling very well. Just as I thought. I knew I had to get it done. So, I got some wallpaper and decorated the children's bedroom. I had carpets installed on the floor and stairs. I continued decorating and Gary wouldn't help me. I was so determined that I had to do this on my own. I just did it. I was still working at the cinema and he then stopped working again. Each time he stopped working, he would go to the pub. I was getting fed up with his lazy attitude. I felt he thought life owed him something. It was very embarrassing for me. I looked like the breadwinner and it looked like I was carrying all of us, which was very true. I really didn't know how much longer I could cope with this.

I spoke with him sometimes about his intentions concerning employment. I felt at one point he wanted me to give up my job and not work. He mentioned we would get more money if we both were on benefits. I would never do that because things are bad now. How would it be if I didn't work? Living off benefits wasn't my style and ambition. I already noticed that he didn't have any ambition to achieve anything in life and I felt he thought life owed him something. I was just done with his laziness and relying on benefits. I felt that if he found a job or went to college to train for something, he would be more motivated and his wellbeing would improve.

One of Gary's friends joined the territorial army and told him about it. He joined up and was accepted. It was good because this meant he would have something else to focus on. He spoke about the training, which was hard and felt happy, especially when he had the uniform on. He walked tall. I hadn't seen him smile like this for a long time. He appeared to be thrilled with a sense of pride. He was very dedicated for a while. Then communication ceased; his moods changed; he became reserved. Each week before his attendance, silence reigned. He later mentioned that there were a few of the guys he couldn't get on with. I felt I had been here before. I last heard that statement with his last job. No one liked him or spoke to him. "Oh God, this is a repeated cycle!" I thought, *Let's see what happens because I know the cycle very well.* Only this time I won't be picking up the pieces.

He was now on benefits. I was still working at the cinema. My day was getting up, making sure that Crystal and Marsha were given breakfast and taken to school, getting back in time to tidy up the house; washing, cleaning and cooking the dinner before I went to work. Gary would stay in bed for most of the day and appeared to sit and watch television all day. Eventually, he complained about how he felt. I knew he had no intention of getting a job. Some days, he would go to the pub and play chess. A few times, he invited this man to the house. My mannerism wasn't very welcoming, so I didn't see him again. This was his lifestyle and he was ok with it.

He became very sharp with me as he complained about the children playing. I found myself watching him, trying not to do much talking. As I knew when he was in one of his moods, I knew what could happen. It really upset me that it had become like this. I saw it as he sat there, staring, as if he were in his own world and nothing and no one existed. I felt very uncomfortable and dared not say anything in case I said the wrong thing. I sometimes thought, *is it me that's wrong?* I felt that our lives should be better than this. I just couldn't allow him to ill-treat the children and think it was ok. I think children need a safe home to feel comfortable enough to play. His headaches and ailments were not the children's fault.

Every time I tried to talk about anything with him, it ended up in an argument. Then he would always say I'm spoiling them. I felt angry and frustrated within and felt trapped between a rock and a hard place. I was carrying this family. His parents never gave me any recognition. I was disappointed and very hurt by how he behaved towards me (short-tempered) and the children (no interest in their development). All he did was eat everything in sight. The snacks and treats I bought for the children disappeared. He had now gained weight. This was his worst nightmare.

The children told me he left them alone in the house whilst I was at work. I was furious. I spoke to him about it, and he said, "I only jog for 30 minutes."

"Where? Why are you so irresponsible?" I asked him.

"The park, for 15 to 30 minutes." He said, thinking nothing of it.

"How could you?" I had such a headache I thought I wanted to be sick. I was so disappointed. "You left our children alone! What on earth were you thinking?" He said nothing and continued watching the TV. He looked very sheepish but said nothing. "How long have you been leaving them?" I felt my body getting hot and took a deep breath as I thought of my beautiful girls being neglected by their own father.

This was shocking. I didn't want to look at him, wondering what I should do. I walked out and headed to the bedroom. I didn't want to see his face. This left me thinking very seriously about my life and things seemed to be getting worse. There was a thought that always came into my mind. Can I really continue to live in misery?

I thought about my issues going to work and coming back. *Am I happy with him? Have I got the energy to continue? Do I love him?* The answer was, "No."

I had put up with his attitude and disrespect toward me in more ways than one. (I wanted to tell my mum what he was doing to me but I didn't want her worried). I had tried. Both of us had the responsibility of looking after our children. I was tired of carrying him. I always made sure the children were taken care of, and the bills and feeding all of us, whilst he chose not to work. "Who is looking after me?" I asked myself. I made my mind up. I had to change my life. If I stayed, I would always be miserable and live in poverty, always borrowing from Peter to pay back Paul (as my mother would say). I wanted to give my children a better life.

I mentioned it to my mum, and she worried aloud, "It will be hard to raise the children alone. If you work, how will you manage everything?"

"God will make a way. I'm going to pray about it. I'm done with his laziness, expecting everything to be given to him on a platter. Watching TV from morning to night. Not bothering about the children watching programmes they like. He never takes them out or has fun with them." I said confidently.

Over the years, he has gone up two sizes. His clothes didn't fit and he had to buy a bigger size. This triggered him off, then he would take it out on the children and me. I was beginning to be concerned about leaving the children alone with him. It was very difficult most of the time to get a normal conversation out of him. Sitting there staring at the television. Shutting the world out. I hardly recognised him. "I have no feelings. I am not happy. I don't know if I will ever be again Mum. That's the truth."

I then noticed Gary becoming more withdrawn, not having much patience with the children and often moody with me.

Sometimes I felt he was going to hit me again. It was becoming very dangerous not knowing what he would do next. I didn't feel safe leaving the children, and everyday things just seemed to get worse.

I tried to help him one day, encouraging him to seek help. He agreed to see a doctor, but there was no improvement. I'd heard of counselling and I told him about it. I only knew that people who had issues with their moods would benefit from the sessions. He didn't want any medication but was put on the counselling waiting list by the doctor. Meanwhile, things at home were very different. I had to speak to Crystal, who was six, letting her know Daddy wasn't feeling too good and she had to be a good girl. I felt I was walking on eggshells and had to be very careful about what I said and how I phrased things. During the weeks ahead, I experienced Gary's attitude towards me. He usually related to me in a very hostile and frustrated manner.

I preferred his taking it out on me rather than on the children. It was becoming a usual thing; him hitting me. I told him, "I'm not your punching bag and if you continue, I will leave you." I remember thinking this would never happen to me, but now it was my reality. I was determined, if he ever raised his hands to me again, I would definitely leave.

I remembered one night he got in one of his moods and began to argue with me about something that he didn't like. I noticed a pattern. He would argue, hit me, and then he would want to make love. (To make things better). I knew that this was not love. He was just taking advantage of me yet again. I was adamant that he was not going to have sex with me that night. Again, he slapped me. This was not making love. He was rough and forced himself on me. (This was abuse). I then made my mind up. Never again will I let him do this to me ever. He was a bully who didn't respect me.

I had never seen him so angry because I had said, "No." According to him, I was his wife and that was my duty. I sensed a lack of respect and humanity in how I was treated; this was my body, after all! He should have loved and cherished me with kindness and gentleness. This was the last time he would put his hands on me.

I went to my mother and father's house and took enough clothes for a while. This was the end of this marriage. I had to be very smart with him as he would try to plead with me to stay or really hurt me. I stayed calm and didn't tell him what my intensions were. I rang in sick at work and told them I wouldn't be back for a week because of a family crisis. The children were asleep throughout this commotion. Thank God they were, they were none the wiser.

The night before decided for me. I will not be a punching bag or be sexually abused. Will not be disrespected by him again. He was acting differently and I was not going to allow this behaviour. He seemed to be furious and doing things out of character. I had to follow my instincts. My gut feelings, deep down, don't lie. I felt I was in danger. It was the right time to leave. Returning home after taking the children to school. The school is very close to my parents' house. I went to my Mum and dad's house to tell them of my plan to leave Gary. I had already mentioned to my mum what my intention was earlier. I know I was a bit later than usual and

I didn't want him to sense anything about leaving him. I had to be calm and vigilant and focused.

I got up as usual and took the children to school. I told them we were going to spend some time at Grandma and grandad's house. Crystal asked, "Why, Mummy?"

"We are going to spend some time with them because they need us to keep them company for a bit. Is that ok with both of you?"

"Yes, Mummy, that's ok."

I visited my Mum and Dad at home to tell them about my plan. I had kept my mother informed regarding the situation I endured. I checked if it would be ok for the children and me to stay with them until I sorted myself out. They welcomed me with open arms; they were also very upset that it had come to this.

I told them we may end up staying a while until the solicitor had sorted everything out. My father wanted to go to the house to speak to him, but I told him I preferred if he didn't.

Returning home, I didn't really know what to expect. He was watching TV as usual. He asked me, "Do you want something to eat?"

"No, thanks."

"You were a bit long getting back. Where did you go?"

"I was speaking to a group of parents at the school regarding the children and their progress."

"Ok, that must have been interesting?"

"Yes, it was actually."

"Well, I'm going to the pub in a minute. You don't mind, do you?"

"Not at all." I felt he was being very nice. I hoped he didn't pick up on anything that I was planning. He got something to eat, had a shower and eventually went to the pub. I watched him as he walked down the street. I then packed. I started praying, as I didn't want him to come back for anything. I felt very frightened, but knew I was doing the right thing for me and the girls.

I started packing as fast as I could. The girls' clothes first, footwear, and coats. Then I started packing my things. Clothes, footwear, and coats. I didn't realise how many clothes we had. There were so many bags. I then called a taxi. I was told it would be 10 minutes. It was the longest 10 minutes I've ever known. I took deep breaths; I could almost hear my heart pounding in my chest. I didn't know what to do with myself at this point. My mind was now racing 90 miles an hour. This is not good. I started praying, "Please God, please don't let him come back. Oh no, now I want the toilet. Oh God, why now?" I ran to the toilet and was constantly listening out for a door to open. What can I do if he comes through the door? Fiercely, I started looking around for something to defend myself. Looking around, I couldn't see anything. Then my mind went blank and I felt sick to my stomach. After leaving the toilet, I ran down the stairs and looked out of the front window. I was so relieved when I heard the taxi driver honk his horn.

I then opened the door, which was locked, and started putting the bags outside the gate. I asked the taxi man, "Can you please help me? I have to leave now!" He then realised what was going on with me. We got the clothes, and then I checked all my documents. Which I left in a bag earlier. Before I left in the morning. I took my passport, bank book, cards, everything of importance that belonged to me and left. I felt much safer because if he came back now, I could call the police before I got to my parent's home and then get the children. I thanked the taxi driver and gave him a tip for his kindness and went inside quickly. I had to sit down to catch my breath. The next place I had to go was the school, to tell the headmaster what I'd done and collect the children.

When I went to collect the children, the headmaster listened and understood what was going on. He told me he could arrange some work to be done at home for a few days.

This was the way I left this marriage.

The next day, he came to school around lunchtime. He saw my father and Marsha, then declared he wanted to see his kids and started pulling Marsha's leg while I was still holding her. My father went up to him and he kicked my father to the ground and my father held on to his feet, but he wriggled and got away. Then he left. I'm glad because if my father had gotten him on the ground, he would have hurt him badly. This left Marsha distorted for days, as she was in the midst of this foolishness. I was glad my dad was with me because he would have really injured me badly. I didn't go back to the house until my solicitor sorted out my rights to return to the home. (It took about four months). He had to leave so that the children had their home back.

He went back home to his mother. He saw me in the street but couldn't approach me or the children. The solicitor helped me go back into the house with the children, as it was a council property. He couldn't claim anything. There was no money. He didn't work for years.

I walked into the house to find it completely stripped; the fridge, sofa, TV, and every other piece of furniture had been removed. The dining room carpet was gone, and all the kitchenware, bedding, and even the blankets had been taken. I couldn't believe it. I just thanked God that we were safe and that it was only things he had taken, not our lives, but things that could be replaced.

The divorce went through quickly and it was a relief for me. I felt I could get on with my life now and bring up the girls in peace and harmony, how it should be. I had to give up my job as my mum was older and couldn't look after the children. I took the girls everywhere, as usual. We had a good, peaceful life. We went to my mum's a lot as I wasn't working. I still felt I had to pursue my dream of being self-sufficient. After thinking about what I wanted to do. I went to college whilst the girls were in school. I studied and got an O Level in English.

8.
CARLOS AGAIN

One day I was visiting my Mum and Dad's. To my surprise, I saw Carlos. I was so glad to see him because I hadn't seen him for years. I asked him, "How are you?"

"I'm fine, thanks. How are you doing?"

"I haven't seen you in years. What you up to?"

"I live over there in that house." He points to a large house on the corner. "I'm living on the first floor. I've been living there for about six months now."

"Ok."

"I'm living opposite your Mum; I sometimes visit her." He said.

"Do you, ok? You look so different and I can't recognise what it is."

"A lot of people tell me that."

"So, what is it, then?"

"I have given my life to the Lord now."

"Ok, that's great. You look so well."

"You can come to church with me if you want to, one Sunday. I go to Harehills Baptist Church." Carlos looked radiant and so happy; I wanted what he had for sure.

"Yes, I will, one Sunday."

"That would be nice." He then asked me, "Are these your children?"

"Yes, this is Crystal. She is six and Marsha is three." From that day on, I saw Carlos in a very different light. I would go to my mum's and he would be there sometimes. We would all have a laugh and Carlos was so funny. He was one of those people who would talk about anything and everything. He enjoyed cooking. Most of the time, he and my parents would speak about preparing and exchanged how they cooked certain dishes. The way Carlos and my mother got on intrigued me. He even got my father laughing. He's the first guy that ever took anytime, to have a conversation with my parents.

Visiting my parents was a joy, but even better. I began hoping he would be there and that afternoon he was. Crystal, Marsha and I went in. I heard his voice, as usual. "Good afternoon, everyone. Is everyone ok?"

I couldn't wait to tell him the news. "By the way, we have decided, haven't we, girls? We are going to church this Sunday."

"Oh great, that is nice," replied Carlos and smiled as he looked at me, then glanced away. I didn't see him again until Sunday at church.

As I opened the door to the church, a man smartly dressed, with a nice smile said, "Hello welcome and led me to some empty chairs in the middle of the church. I was very conscious of holding onto Crystal and Marsha's hands as I sensed their nervousness and felt people watching us as we sat down. I looked at Carlos in amazement. I didn't expect to see him on the stage.

After church I asked Carlos, "Why didn't you tell me you played the drums?"

"Oh, I used to play the drums for artists in bands. I play the drums for the Lord now."

I was so touched by this. I looked at him and saw a man of substance. Later, he told me he had played with many of the well-known bands in England. I was impressed and noticed he would find anything to practise his drumming. Halfway through the service Carlos asked me if the girls wanted to go to Sunday school. "Yes, I'll come with you," I replied, and followed Carlos and the girls into a hall.

All the children were put in groups according to their ages. Both Crystal and Marsha were in different groups. I made sure they were ok, then Carlos and I went back in to hear the sermon. Sitting together was rather strange. The minister spoke. The silence was so different; in the calmness there was a warmth that I didn't experience. I could have cried at that moment. The words that were expressed resonated with me. How can I do everything on my own? I needed help. I needed God to change my way of thinking and to change my life completely. I really believed every word. Looking around the church, I saw people wiping their eyes, listening, absorbing attentively. The minister spoke with a calm, sincere voice, looking around at everyone, concentrating with a sense of knowledge and authority. It was so different from what I'm used to. He would look down occasionally at his notes but looked up at everyone, speaking with so much passion and sincerity. It felt wonderful to my ears. I was so touched by this reassuring message. Something happened within me. At the end of the sermon, the minister asked the congregation if they wanted Jesus to be their Saviour, they should come to the altar and he would pray with them. This was a new experience for me. A few people went up. I really wanted to go to the front but didn't. I left the church accompanied by Carlos, his son Paul and the girls. We attended church every week after that. The girls enjoyed going and made friends.

One morning, I walked to the front of the church and gave my life to Christ. This was the first time of not worrying about anyone else. I knew I wanted to do this for me. Making that decision was the best thing I have ever done for myself. I felt lighter, freer, happier, and felt loved by my Heavenly Father and knew if I died, I would go to be with my creator. I felt the change within. I wanted to tell everyone about my experience and I told everyone who asked me the same thing I asked Carlos, There is something about you, but I can't put my finger on it. For about two years, Carlos and I were very good friends.

The children and I would get up and dance to Carlos' drumming. He was an excellent drummer.

Myself and the girls, Carlos, and his son Paul, who was a few years younger than Crystal. We went to church each week. It was a joy to be in Carlos's company. His passion for God intrigued me. He was funny, polite and kind, towards the children and me. After church, we would go to my parents' house. Also, we were invited to other church members' houses, which was really nice. We developed a great relationship. It was so nice to speak about our faith, and what issues came up for us. Thursday was group meeting. My mum would have the girls on Thursdays after school, then I would take them to school on Friday mornings. Group meeting was the place to share anything that we found difficult, pray, build each other up, when things were rocky. Praise him for everything. Carlos came around one evening. I told him that Gary had gotten a visitation notice to see the girls every fortnight. I felt very resentful, as he did nothing with them before. Was he trying to get back at me or did he really want to see them?

I kept Gary at the door. It was very difficult, knowing he would have the children every fortnight. Crystal always wanted her dad's approval, love, and was eager to see him. Marsha wasn't bothered at all. I got them both ready. Crystal was telling Marsha, "Hurry because Dad is here now!" and Marsha would sit there with her fingers in her mouth, telling Crystal that she didn't want to go. I saw a division between them. After a while, Gary started to look smart, as if he went to church. I was surprised when Crystal told me he'd actually started going to church. When he came to pick them up, I looked out of the bedroom window, trying not to make myself visible. The girls would go and the door would close. When they returned the same method, in reverse. This went on for some time.

For about two years, Carlos and I were very good friends. We spoke about taking our relationship to the next level. I was still very apprehensive after my marriage and left scared for a long time. The girls were now eight and five yrs old. Carlos and I became a couple. We took things slowly because of the children and of the way I felt at this time. I liked Carlos a lot. I had just got divorced and wasn't ready to make that commitment. Yet, there was no doubt in my head that I had fallen for Carlos. It was complicated and I felt we could wait and pray. I just didn't want to jeopardise our relationship that was working. We were happy and we came to an agreement, both of us together. I'd grown to love Carlos so much. He had so many qualities. When I was struggling with anything, he listened and was very sensitive in his response. He was honest with his thoughts and would allow me to be emotional, telling me, "Things will work out." I really trusted him; he was so different from the children's father. I didn't have to be careful of what I said or did. He made me laugh all the time. We shared the cooking, cleaned the house together. We didn't argue but had times of silence. I would look at him and he would pretend not to look at me. I would continue looking at him. He would make comments in a Caribbean accent like, "Why you watching me like dat girl?" I would laugh and he would smile. If I was wrong, I would apologise, then talk about it if it were the right time or discuss it another time. Being around Carlos was very peaceful, without stress and fear. He was easy-going and helpful to me and the children. At this time, Carlos wasn't working but he was very different from Gary. Carlos helped me in many ways.

9.
THE ACCIDENT

Emma, an old friend of mine, who I grew up with, had a salon and suspected the receptionist was stealing the takings. She came to my mother's house to ask if I would be interested in filling the position on Saturdays only. We then agreed on the wages. I then accepted.

I discussed childcare arrangements with Carlos. "Yes, Vee, I will if you want me to. You know they will be safe with me, darling."

"Will it be ok though babes, are you really sure?"

"Yes, darling, it will be fine."

"I really thank you for this, darling."

"It's a big ask, though, babes."

"You know I will look after them." He assured me.

I thought, *He would be the ideal person to look after the girls while I was at work. All I had to do was ask him?* He didn't hesitate and said, "Yes, I can, if you want me to. I thought about how kind and thoughtful that was. To be prepared to look after both Crystal and Marsha leave at 8.30am on Saturdays. My role was to collect the money from the customers only.

On my first day, Emma introduced me to her staff. I was welcomed and enjoyed the job. After a few weeks, I heard some of the staff speaking about Emma in an unpleasant manner. I pretended not to hear but couldn't understand that they were talking about the same person. One day I experienced the way Emma spoke to one of her staff in front of the whole salon. I felt really sorry for this person as she was near tears. I continued working for Emma until one day, before getting to work, I nearly lost my life.

One Saturday morning. Going to the salon. I was going to catch the bus. As I was early, I crossed the road. As I stood in the middle of the road, I could see a car on my left side. I waited for him to turn right. I saw the car coming straight at me. I thought I was going to die that morning. Everything went into slow motion. I saw the car coming my way. I remembered shouting, "Oh God, is this how I'm going to die? Then, the car hit me. I felt my body turning around in the air, then fell onto the front of the car. The force of the impact then caused me to fall to the ground. The engine stopped, then I heard the engine rev. I saw a wheel coming toward me. I thought I had to tighten my stomach as hard as I could, so if the wheel went over my stomach, it wouldn't splash out. As the wheel went over my stomach, I was surprised it felt light.

The car suddenly stopped, but then started revving up again. I thought if this car runs over me again, I will die. I then rolled from right to left, looking at the wheel under the car. I was between the four wheels. I started rolling left and right to prevent them from rolling over me. This person in the car wanted to run over me again. I did this several times. When I saw peoples, legs standing in front of the car screaming, "You're going to kill her! "Stop the car! Stop the car!" and the car engine stopped. I was so frightened; I pulled myself from under the car. I ran into the shop, which the people had left, to save me.

Running into the shop. I was breathless, frightened, thoughts of what had happened. The shop owner said, "Oh my God, are you ok?"

"He was trying to kill me! He nearly killed me..."

The owner exclaimed, "I'm going to call the police!" After a short wait, the ambulance came and took me to a street close by and asked me questions and examined me.

I told them what had happened.

"How are you feeling?"

"I'm just shocked that this man tried to kill me."

"After examining you, it doesn't seem like you have any broken bones. I must tell you that if the owner of the shop didn't tell us what had happened, I wouldn't have believed you. You have no broken bones! I still need to take you to the hospital for a second opinion, though. Someone's looking over you." He said with a smile.

"Yes, I know it's God."

Arriving at the hospital. The whole incident came back to me. I could see this man's face in the car. He looked like he was Jewish or Italian. He had an olive skin type. I didn't recognise or know him.

My eyes widen noticeably. Everything looked dazzling and clearer than usual. I heard people's voices louder. It was strange. Very worrying, I've never experienced this before. In the distance, I saw my mother. Seeing her so upset and concerned. I didn't want to make her feel worse.

"Lord Ronnie, how are you feeling, darling?"

"How did you know about this, Mum? I asked.

"The police came to the house and told me." Mum's tears were rolling down her cheeks.

"Mum don't cry, I will be ok, Mum. God has this in his hands. I politely asked the porter, "Could you stop for a moment, please?"

I called my Mum over and held her close and kissed her on her cheeks and forehead. Then they took me into a room. All I could think about was my mother crying in the waiting area. I asked a nurse if my Mum could come in with me. I just didn't want Mum to worry or not speak to anyone for hours.

She was still very upset; I tried to console her but it made me feel even worse seeing her crying. I was examined. I told the doctor how my eyes felt and my hearing. The doctor told me I was feeling like this because of shock. They had arranged for my doctor to visit me for seven days at home.

I then thought of my neighbour opposite, whose daughter had died of a brain clot a few days ago, leaving a baby behind. I prayed continually and thanked my Heavenly Father for saving me and sparing my life to continue bringing up my children. After some time, I was taken home. When I arrived home, my oldest sister Isabella was sweeping the stairs. She greeted me. "How are you feeling?"

"I'm not too bad. I haven't broken any bones, so that's good."

"Yes, it is you go and get some rest". I got a shock. Isabella was sweeping up. *Does she know something I don't?* I felt my sister may know more about what was wrong with me. I felt so unwell. Why was she sweeping up and tidying up? What did that mean? Were people descending upon the house? It made me think. *Am I going to be ok or I'm I going to die?* I didn't feel connected to my body. I felt my spirit absent from my body. It was on the outside, waiting to get back inside me.

I hugged the children. I was overwhelmed with happiness to see them. I hugged and kissed them both at the same time. They cried. I knew they'd been crying by their puffy eyes. They asked me if I would be ok. "Of course, my babies, I have to look after you both, don't I?" Then they smiled.

Carlos was at the door but I knew he wouldn't hug or show any affection whilst my mother or sister were there. We watched each other. He looked concerned and worried.

"Hi, how are you feeling?", asked Carlos.

"I'm not too bad. Just a bit tired."

He then said, "I'll help you get washed and dressed."

"Yes, thanks.", I replied.

I needed some time with Carlos. I needed him to console me. He guided me upstairs to the bathroom. He undressed, showered me and put my nighty on. At this time, I just wanted to go to bed. Carlos helped me into bed. He sat next to me. I started crying. He hugged and kissed me. As I sobbed, he reassured me I would be ok. He always made me feel better. To be in his arms meant so much. He was always gentle and considerate towards me, which caused me to melt into his arms.

"Oh, babes, how are you feeling?" said Carlos.

"I feel strange. My eyes feel really big and everything appears so bright. When people are speaking, it sounds really loud. I told the doctor and they examined me." I continued to explain what had happened whilst I could remember. "I hit my head on the car before I hit the ground. The doctor said, the GP will visit me from tomorrow."

"Ok, I'm so glad you're home. I've been praying for you, darling. It's great to have you back. I was so worried when I heard what happened, because you had just left home when the police came and told me. I know everything happened so quickly. I just couldn't believe it. How are the girls? I had to tell them you had an accident. They cried and wanted to see you. They were very upset, asking if you were coming back home. I told them, "Of course; Mummy has to come back to all of us."

"I knew you would help them understand. Thank you." I didn't want this moment to end.

I felt a moment of gratitude as he looked into my eyes and said, "I'm so thankful you're ok, I was so worried. I'm so glad you're here, darling." Carlos replied. I felt myself drifting and a warm feeling came over me. I was so grateful I was still alive. Carlos continued to hold me and, for the first time, I saw his eyes filling up. I was bewildered. Not knowing what to do, I started crying. Carlos held me tight and told me, "God is with you Vee, you know that. You will be ok Vee. I will look after you, darling. Don't worry, I'm here. I will look after the children, so don't worry; you know they will be ok darling."

"I wish we could be together tonight; I just want you to hold me."

"Your mum wants to stay and it's only right for her to sleep with you babes."

"Yes. That's true."

"We are all worried about you. I will be up early in the morning to take the children to school and then spend all day with you."

Reassured, I then went to sleep.

Before I knew it, it was morning. Mum got up out of bed and asked me, "Do you want something to eat, Ronnie?"

"I don't know, Mum." I replied.

"You have to eat something, Ronnie; I will bring you up some cornflakes or porridge. Which one?"

"Ok mum can I have some cornflakes please, just a little please, Mum." Mum disappeared with her clothes and her towel and toothbrush in her hand. I closed my eyes and must have dropped off.

Then I heard Carlos' gentle voice saying, "Babes, how are you feeling today?"

I said, "I'm feeling exhausted, darling."

Carlos said, "I have bought you something to eat." I tried to get up but found it hard to move. Carlos helped me to sit up. He rearranged my pillows to make me comfortable, then fed me cornflakes. I watched him as he gently fed me. I couldn't have a lot, as I was feeling so unwell. I slid back underneath the sheets and went to sleep. The doctor came and gave me an injection later on and every day after. I was told it would be for a week.

People came to visit. The room seemed lengthy, with everyone gathered at one end. One visitor was my sister Melda, who brought me up from the West Indies. I told her, "I'm not going to die, because Jesus told me." I constantly heard heavenly music. One night I saw the outline of a person sideways looking at me from the bottom of the bed. I told my mum. Who replied, "Stop saying these things and go to sleep."

"Mum, there's a person sitting at the side of the bed." I said to the person, "If you're of God, I welcome you, but if you're not, I want you to go, in Jesus' name." This person was wearing a turban and a robe and sat looking at me. A sense of peace was in the room. "He's still here, Mum." The person and I both looked at each other.

Waking up the next morning. Thinking about what I saw last night. I looked out of the window. I turned around and could see someone in the distance. It was as if the room had become longer than usual. I saw people coming into the room in slow motion. Some faces I recognised and some I didn't. I felt I was also drifting. Looking out of the window, I saw a cloud in the form of the face of Jesus, and different shapes. One of a harp, the other doves. This was fascinating, watching them drift by. I was drifting too. It was so calm and peaceful. I thought of the children. Where are they? I wanted to see them but didn't have the energy to shout. I then started praying. "God, please don't let me die. What will happen to the children?"

I was lost in time, not knowing what day it was, when the drifting motions began to slowly stop. I couldn't believe how long I had been ill. As time passed, I realised how ill I was. I was told that I was in a serious position, as the shock could have caused death.

10.
FRIGHTENED

Carlos took the children to and from school. I was very scared of the sound of cars. The sound of joyriders revving their engines would bring tears to my eyes. No one could get me out of the house. I wouldn't even look out of the window. It was summer and no one saw me at all.

One day my cousin, who I call sister Loretta, came to take me out. She asked, "Why don't you want to go out?" She convinced me to just walk to the first block of my street and then we would walk back if I wanted to. I was frightened to go outside. Sister Loretta helped me to put my shoes and jacket on. She promised to hold my hand all the way there and back. I agreed after a while of persuasion. Taking deep breaths.

I got to the open door. I felt scared and unwell. I wanted to be sick. Sister Loretta held my hand and guided me out of the house and locked the door. She reassured me she would hold my hand throughout. I stopped at the gate. The sight of the cars made my stomach feel sick. Suddenly, I didn't know how I was going to do this task. It was the hardest thing I had ever had to do. She opened the gate and this was my worst nightmare. She held on to me and I was holding on to her tightly. We walked a few steps, then I heard a car. I put my hands over my face. I just didn't know what to do. Walking a bit more, it was still difficult but doable. We eventually got to the end of the block. I held her as she encouraged me to continue to the end of my street. Then sister Loretta took me back home. I was so thankful to her for her kindness and patience. Sister Loretta came back the next day, as planned, to walk me to her house. Her house was five minutes' walk away. After a while, I was able to go out on my own. I will always be grateful to my sister Loretta for helping when I really needed encouragement. The children were only five and eight yrs old. Carlos took them to school and collected them and cooked and looked after me and the children. I could now go out on my own. It took me six weeks. I have never seen this man before. Up to this day, I don't know why. The case went to court and he had to pay me compensation. I was devastated and terrified for six weeks. I couldn't look out of the windows, too frightened to see a car pass by. I became very depressed. I couldn't go out to take the children to school.

11

RETURNING TO WORK

I got the impression that Emma had changed. I felt Emma didn't need me anymore and she didn't know how to tell me. So, she spoke to me differently. She forgot I knew her before her shop's success inflated her ego. Being gone for six weeks. Emma had other plans for me. One day, I asked her. "Will you teach me hairdressing?"

"No, because your father will open up a salon and you will be successful. I'm thinking of opening a gym. You would be good at that."

"No. I'm not a gym person."

At work, I noticed Emma was very stern and ruthless with the staff. This was a side I had never seen before. Some of the staff were very hesitant when speaking to her. The atmosphere was very uncomfortable. The clients would watch on whilst someone was told off. Emma would say, "Make some teas! Why are you standing there? Haven't you got anything else to do? If not, clean the mirrors. Until one day she did it to me.

The salon was very busy. As I looked on at my friend and her stylist working, I heard a loud shout. "Can't you see there are cups that need to be taken up, and the floor needs sweeping?" I was shocked with unbelief. Was she speaking to me? I looked at her with an eyebrow, raised, mouth cracked.

I stood there and asked, "Who are you talking to? Are you speaking to me?"

"Yes, you!" I didn't say another word and began collecting the cups, then swept the floor. As I was collecting the cups and sweeping the floor, I was thinking about the whole process. I couldn't feel my legs. The room became still. No one spoke. All eyes were on me. I felt a warm feeling, a sensation in my stomach. I wanted to say something, but I held it. Anger was rising within me. I took another look at the faces looking back at me. I had become even smaller than before. What can I do now to take all these feelings away? I started to breathe very slowly and tried not to express any embarrassment. Telling myself, *It's ok Emma. You're doing this because you think you can.* I could feel my hands shaking and a sick feeling came into my stomach.

In the changing room. Everyone was busy getting ready to go home. I said, "Emma, I would like to say something to you."

She watches me from the corner of her eye. "Yes, about what?"

"Why did you speak to me that way in front of everyone earlier? These people don't know you like I do. Growing up as kids. You ate food off my plate, and we both would jump on my mother's bed. We didn't have much, but you had even less than I. It's a shame when people forget where they're coming from. Don't speak like that to me again, ever."

All of her staff looked at her. She glanced at me. The room went quiet, and she said nothing. I then got my belongings and returned to the reception area. Walking towards me. She didn't look at me but began to check the tab receipts. Then she opened the till and checked the takings. "Is all the money there?" I asked her defiantly.

"Yes," she replied. "It's correct."

"Great."

"I'm letting you go tonight."

"Are the takings right?" I asked for the second time.

"Yes, I said it is." Emma replied.

"That's great." I said and left. I felt she thought I was below her. At the time wasn't working and she felt I was not going nowhere, so she felt she could speak to me anyhow. I felt belittled by a person I thought was my friend. Unfortunately, it allowed me to see her true colours and how having more finance than me at the time gave her the power to make me feel I didn't matter. It opened my eyes to see how some people can change because of their financial status. I told myself after that incident that I will never become like that ever. No matter what I have or do not have to be contented with a little and with a lot. Money can make people change for the better or for the worse. I want to be the best I can be, with or without. I just aspire to be contented in my life and help others along my journey.

Marsha is very good at singing. My mum said that Marsha had a voice like my dad's grandmother, who used to sing in church. When my grandmother sang, the whole community would come to the church to hear her. The church was full and people would be outside listening to her. Apparently, great grandma had the voice of an angel. Marsha and her friend Zara practised for months for a competition. Marsha asked her father to support her, only to be told he wouldn't come due to his being in the church. I felt it was a poor excuse. Having children is about helping them develop, being supportive and encouraging them, and believing in their talent. He didn't go.

I then saw Emma, who hadn't spoken to me for years, until this event. My daughter was competing in a singing competition. I was selling tickets for the raffle. Emma approached me, saying, "Your daughter has a lovely voice."

"Oh, thank you." I replied and moved on.

12.

TEACH ME HAIRDRESSING

Losing my job made me more determined to be a hairdresser. After speaking to my mother regarding what happened with Emma. My mother mentioned it to one of her close friends. Who'd been a client of this woman for a very long time. She told her what had happened. (Growing up, I had to give older people a title such as Miss, Mr, Aunty, or Uncle. I couldn't call them by their name without the title at the beginning). Miss Evie asked her hairdresser if she would teach me hairdressing. She said she would see me to discuss what I needed. I was over the moon, but very apprehensive about meeting her. God, you did it again.

The appointment was made. Going to her house, I didn't know what to expect. Will I like her? Will she like me? Could we work together? Is she as good as Miss Evie says? All these questions went through my head. Oh God, I'm here. I took some deep breaths and whispered to myself, "God, please let this person be ok."

I approached the door and rang the doorbell. The door opened and there was a very smart woman, who greeted me with a broad smile that seemed friendly. "Hello, come in. How are you?"

"I'm fine, thank you." I replied. I was taken into the kitchen area. The kitchen was very tidy. Everything put away. "

"You can sit down." She said as she pointed to a chair. "Would you like a drink of tea, coffee, or water?" she asked.

"Yes, please. Can I have some water?"

"Sure, that's fine," she replied. She got the water and sat down opposite me. "Evie told me about you. I told we can meet and then take thinks from there."

"What is your name?" she asked.

"My name is Veronica. What is your name?"

"My name is Ruth; most people call me Ruthy."

"What would you like me to call you?"

She laughed and said, "Ruthy.".

"That's great. So, I will remember that easily, Ruthy." I replied.

"I understand you want to be a hairdresser?" Said Ruthy.

"Yes, I do. I was working in a salon for about nine months as a receptionist. I was responsible for the takings. In working there, I was inspired. I wondered, could I do this? I loved the creativity of the stylists and seeing people going out happy with their new looks.

I asked the owner if she would teach me hairdressing. She refused and told me she wanted me to run a gym for her instead. I told her I'm not a gym person. I had to do what was best for me;" I replied.

"Well, that's right. We all have to do what is right for ourselves." Ruthy replied. "I studied in America; the course was for two years. I was taught the theory and practice in Black hair and European hair in America. I lived there for several years after completing the course. Then came back to the UK and opened her hairdressing salon. I had a salon for several years and closed it because the costs went up so high. I am now working from home. Most of her customers still get their hair done. Speaking with Ruthy was a refreshing experience. She allowed me to ask questions. I got to know her passion for hairdressing. How she cared for her client's wellbeing and recommended products for home care. After the meeting, I understood so much. She explained things so easily. She seemed very dedicated to hairdressing. I felt very excited. "What do you think, Veronica?"

"I would love for you to teach me, Ruthy. What you have shared with me has made me feel very excited about starting this course with you." Then she agreed she would like to teach me hairdressing.

Ruthy told me the course would be for one year. "You will have to get your folder and invest in a book that you will learn from. I will get it from America." Ruthy told me about her fee, the hours we would meet every week. She outlined to me what I would learn. I would get a certificate at the end to prove I had attended. "I have to tell you I'm very serious about teaching anyone, as I expect you to be serious also. It will not be easy. If you want something enough, you will persevere and push through anything to acquire your goal."

Ruthy had a salon for many years. She is well known in the area. I have heard others speak about her but never met her until now. "Thank you so much for seeing me and agreeing to teach me the skills of hairdressing." We spoke about the course and what it entailed. Near the end of the conversation, I asked her questions about her salon experiences and why she went to America to learn hairdressing. She said, "I wasn't impressed with the hairdressers' skills in the UK. I visited America and found a school that specialised in both African/Caribbean & European hair." Ruthy continued, saying, "Being trained properly is important not just for the stylist but also for the clients. When they see improvements in their hair's texture and condition, they always rebook for further appointments."

We agreed to begin within six weeks. We said our goodbyes and Ruth agreed to order the book from America and call me when it arrived.

After leaving the meeting, I was eager to tell Mum, Carlos, and the children. Excited about this new path. Not even in my wildest dreams did I ever imagine being a hairdresser. God, you've done it again. I couldn't wait to begin my course. Ruthy came across as positive, dedicated, and with a passion for hairdressing. After getting home, I told Carlos about meeting Ruthy. "She seems very nice and welcoming. She comes across as very dedicated and educated, regarding hairdressing.

"Ok, is she someone you think you can trust?"

"Ruthy appears genuine and trustworthy. She told me a few things that made me believe she is genuine. When we spoke about the fees, she told me it may be hard for me as I have children. She is willing to spread out the payments. She is getting a contract for us both to sign. Including what she will teach me and in what order."

The first month's training includes shampooing, styling, perms, relaxers, cuts, treatments, and plaiting. You will practise on the mannequin first for each unit before going on to clients. When you have demonstrated and mastered the techniques, then you would carry out the techniques on client and would be supervised throughout until you have achieved the standard and understood the theory. To achieve the requirements. I would say possibly seven months, depending on your understanding of the theory and practical work.

"What do you think?" I asked Carlos.

"It sounds ok, but you need to think about, what days, starting and finishing times. Make sure you are given enough time to pass the course."

"The course is for one year."

'Ok, if she is not feeling well, will she give you that time back?"

"This is why I love you, because you think about things I may miss."

"There is a lot to think about. But the most important thing is, I will be here to look after the girls," said Carlos as he served me my dinner.

"Thanks, darling, this looks fantastic," as I looked at the curry goat and rice and salad on the plate. Carlos was an excellent cook. I looked at him in amazement.

At this time, Carlos was not working, but he helped me so much with the girls, and we shared what we had. We would take it in turn to cook. We would both clean the house. He taught the girls and their friend how to play cricket in the back street. He was the dad that every child would want. Carlos was kind and taught all the kids who wanted to play cricket.

I was usually in the house sewing dresses for the girls and myself. I couldn't afford to buy dresses for them often. I was very good at sewing so I would sew two dresses a week for the children to wear to church on Sunday. Everyone would admire them as I dressed both of them in the same material and style.

We were all happy and enjoyed the life we had. It was a peaceful home, with lots of laughter and jokes, which Carlos would tell us. The children had a kind man and they began to love Carlos as I did. The time of the course came around quickly. Carlos would take the girls to school on the days I went to Ruthy's. I would get home around 8pm. It was a long day but I was enjoying the course. There was so much to learn. When I go home, Carlos would have made sure the girls were washed and in bed by 8pm. He would always have dinner ready for me each time. He wouldn't eat until I came in, but I told him not to wait, as I may be late getting home sometimes.

I left the house at 9.30am until 8pm. I would walk home, as it wasn't too far from where I lived. On the first day, I was very excited and apprehensive. Not knowing what to expect. I rang the bell. Ruthy opened the door. "Good morning, Ruthy," I said. "How are you today?"

"I'm fine. How are you?" Ruthy replied. "Do you want a cup of tea?"

"No, thanks. I'm ok for now. Thank you," I replied.

Ruthy took up a book and handed it to me. "This is your book from America."

"Oh, thank you so much," I started opening the book. I then gave Ruthy the first payment for the course. She gave me a receipt. Ruthy began telling me what we were going to look at for today and for the month. She also had the same book and explained the job and the responsibilities of a hairdresser. I found it fascinating. Ruthy was very good at explaining things I didn't understand. As the day went by, I had a lunch break of half an hour. Then continued with the course. At the end of the evening, I felt I had learnt so much. I left at 7.30pm that first day. Ruthy was very helpful and patient when I needed her to explain anything I wasn't sure about.

When I got home, Carlos had made sure the girls had eaten and washed and were asleep. Carlos would ask me, "Are you ready for your dinner now, darling?" I would feel my chest open up with such warmth for this man. I would just look at his smile and soft voice. "How was your day, Vee?"

"It was very good, babes. It went very well. Ruthy explains things I don't understand. I find that very helpful. She knows her stuff. My days are Tuesdays, Wednesdays, and Thursdays, from 9.30 until 8pm.

"Ok, that's fine."

Over a long period, I developed a close working and personal friendship with Ruthy. Ruthy shared a house with a lady called Sandra. I began to really respect and like both of them. Ruthy began to leave me in the house to go to the doctors or shopping whilst I studied and practised my work. It felt like a home from home. Ruthy accepted me as a daughter and I accepted her as my Mum. She and Sandra were very nice to me and trusted me completely. I then started to treat Ruthy's client's hair. They also liked me and trusted me. Sometimes I wouldn't get home until very late, from 10pm to 11pm, because of working on Ruthy's clients. Ruthy began to give me dinner, because she was really beginning to accept me as her daughter. I also began to love them both, Ruthy and Sandra, as my mothers. They had distinct characters, which made them unique.

When I got home, Carlos was still up, waiting for me. I told him Ruthy gave me dinner. "I'm not hungry tonight, darling."

Carlos said, "It's ok", we can use it tomorrow. He looked at me and asked me, "Are you ok? I was worried when it got so late."

"Sorry, babes, I knew you would be worried." I did Ruthy's client, who had a perm and colour. The waiting between each procedure has to be 30minutes to process. It took so long.

"As long as you're ok darling."

"I'm fine." He was sitting on the settee watching TV. He seemed quiet tonight. "Oh, babes." I went over to him. I hugged and kissed him. He pulled me towards him and I sat on his knee.

He held me tight. "Oh, I missed you so much today. When I didn't see you and it was getting late. I became worried. I feel better now. You're here safe." I turned and looked at him and kissed him again. Carlos had his arms around my waist. It felt so good.

I whispered, "I love you, Carlos. Thank you for being you. I really appreciate you. Thanks for being here for me and the children. Sorry I was so late tonight."

"It's ok, I was worried because you're never this late."

"After the client went, Ruthy told me that the client was very pleased. She was also pleased."

"As long as you're enjoying it, and the clients are happy, that's great."

"Yes, I was really pleased when Ruthy told me that. Oh darling, because of you, I'm able to do this course. I love you!" I exclaimed as I wrapped my arms around his neck and looked into his light brown eyes. I felt his warm body close to mine. We kissed and then looked into each other's eyes. That made me shy. I looked away and he guided my face back towards him and our eyes met again. Carlos had lovely light brown eyes that you rarely see.

As he looked at me, he said, "This is not a one-way street, you know; I love you too." A warm sensation went through my body. His arms around my waist made me feel so safe and special. Then we went upstairs.

The following day. I got up early to see the children. I told them how much I loved and missed them. "How have you both been? How's school?"

Crystal answered, "It's ok Mummy."

"And how are you, Crystal?"

"I'm ok."

"I miss you," said Marsha.

"I miss you too, darling. Guess who is taking you to school today? I am. That's why today I'm helping you to dress and give you breakfast. You know Mummy is learning hairdressing now. That's why Uncle Carlos looks after you and takes you to school sometimes. Have you both been good girls for Uncle Carlos?"

"Yes," said Marsha.

"I have too," replied Crystal.

"That's very good, girls. I'm very proud of you." I made sure I had fun with them whilst we made our way to school, running, and making jokes with each other.

As we approached the school gates, Marsha said, "Will you be in when we come home?"

"Yes, because I'm collecting you from school later."

"I want Uncle Carlos to come too."

"Oh, I think we will let Uncle Carlos have a rest this afternoon. I'm coming for you." I took them to their classes and waved goodbye.

On Returning from taking the girls to school, I went into the bedroom to find Carlos sleeping. I went downstairs into the kitchen to see what was needed for dinner today. It appeared that Carlos had already bought the meat and ingredients for dinner. I smiled, thinking about how thoughtful Carlos was. I made him and myself a cup of tea and headed upstairs. As I entered the bedroom, Carlos was awake. I bent down and gave him a kiss. "Hi babes, did you have a good sleep?"

"Yes, ok"

"Good. I didn't wake you, did I Carlos?"

"No, are you coming back to bed for a bit?"

'Do you want me to?"

"Yes."

"Ok I will." Going back into bed was great. We sipped our tea as we spoke. It was nice just being together. Carlos told me how the girls have been. They would have their moments with each other. At times, they would upset each other. Carlos told me how he handled their fallings out. He would speak to them and try to find out who was in the wrong to get a solution. Then explained why they shouldn't fight or argue. They listened to him and got along with him very well. Anytime they wouldn't do as they were told, Carlos would say, "Ok, I will tell your mum when she comes home." They wouldn't want me to know they were being naughty at all.

Carlos told me after their dinner, they would wash themselves, then have supper, and then he would read them a story before bed. Carlos was a wonderful man. I can't ever remember their father reading to them or playing out in the back street or taking them to the park. Yet Carlos did all these things with them. When they spoke about Carlos, I sensed they were comfortable with him. When I'm at home and he is outside, teaching and playing cricket with them. I can see how they interact with him. There was respect, so they listened to him and followed his instructions. Not just Crystal and Marsha, but all the children. There was laughter, excitement, and fun. I wasn't worried about them whilst I was on this course. I had the most respect for Carlos and was always grateful.

As time went on, it was almost at the end of the course. I felt I had gained the skills to be a good hairdresser. Ruthy didn't give me my certificate until she felt I had earned it. I didn't ask for the certificate either. When she gave me my certificate, I felt that I had now achieved what I needed to move forward. Ruthy continued to let me work on her clients whilst she watched and oversaw the skills I had acquired. I then told people I was a hairdresser. I started to have my own clients. The news went around quickly. I then did people's hair at home to build up my clientele. After some time, the girls were eight years and five years. I started perming Carlos's hair, which also advertised and promoted me as a hairdresser.

I continued to pursue my dream. I found a course for beginners. A nearby college offered an advanced course, which I sought to pursue. I felt it would be very beneficial for me to learn the European side of hairdressing. I asked Ruthy and she agreed with my decision.

I thought this would allow me to broaden my knowledge of European hair. To my surprise, I had learned most of the procedures that were being taught in the class. One day we were taught to do setting. I started setting this client's hair. The tutor, Annie, asked me, "Veronica, are you a hairdresser?" Then I told her I had learned hairdressing but needed a City & Guilds certificate. That is why I applied for this course. The tutor said, "Can you bring in your portfolio tomorrow?" '

"Yes, I can," I replied.

The next day, Annie said, "Having looked at your portfolio, it seems you have to move to the higher class. The next day, she told me she had asked for me to be transferred to the advanced class, which was once a week for one year. I was over the moon. The class was very challenging. We learned to understand product usage completely, knowing when and how to apply our skills and knowledge to solve problems. Acquiring a deeper knowledge of colouring, cuts and different techniques in perms and styling the hair. I enjoyed the course so much. We had to learn the skills of how to open a salon, which included health & safety for clients and staff. How to deal with situations if the client came back with any queries or allergies and how to prevent this happening. The course was very intense, but enjoyable.

This allowed me to gain an Advanced Certificate in Hair & Beauty in City & Guilds. the children were older; they could look after themselves. All I had to do was make sure they had breakfast and got to school. This course equipped me to reach out even more towards my goal of opening my own salon. To achieve this, I applied for a job in engineering. In order to save enough money to open my salon and then buy my house, I prayed about getting this job and the interview was so easy. I got the job. I then knew this was a new chapter of my life. The plan was to buy my house and simultaneously open a saloon. I need this job to sustain me to achieve my goal.

My oldest sister, Isabella, worked there. The company was called Brays. I told Ruthy about it as she knew someone who had worked there too. I got an interview. I was very nervous as I said I wouldn't work in a factory. Now I was eating my own words. My mother would say, never say never. My factory job was temporary; I needed the money for my salon and house.

As I sat there waiting for the interview, all I could think was, *God help me get this job, so I can better my lifestyle for the girls and myself.*

I was called into the office. My intense nervousness subsided after I prayed. Steven, who interviewed me, was friendly and put me at ease, which I was really thankful for. "So why do you want this job, Veronica?"

"I was told that there were some job vacancies and thought I would apply for a job."

"Have you ever worked in engineering before?"

"No, I haven't but I'm willing to learn, Steven."

"Why do you want to work here?"

"I also would like the experience of doing something completely different from anything I have ever done. It's close to home. I have two children so I will walk home and get to them quicker, without waiting for a bus." During the interview, I felt at ease and I answered the questions honestly."

At the end of the interview, Steven told me, "I would like to offer you the job. That's if you want it."

"Yes. I do,"

'Good'. Then he told me about the schedule, my responsibilities, the holidays, and my pay. I accepted and he explained the date to start and the time he needed me to start work. He said he would post all the details and I would start in two weeks. I thanked him. We shook hands and I left. I was thrilled and thought, *God, you have done it again, thank you.*

I worked at this company for three years. Whilst working, I took driving lessons. I didn't pass the first time. I did on the second time. I was over the moon. This was a significant achievement for me as now I could drive and get to my destinations quickly. I just needed to buy a car.

Not long after passing my driving test, I went to the bank and took some money out of my savings. When I got home, I said, "Hello girls, stand in the middle of the room for a minute." They did as I asked, then I tossed the money from my bag over them. They were so happy. "Right now, pick them up, girls, every note. That's for our car." The next day, I bought the car, a Vauxhall Chevette. We were all so happy. It made everything so much easier, shopping, going to church, doing fun things we were in our element.

Carlos and I were still very close. I sometime thought he became very quiet when Gary's name was mentioned. Gary got permission from the court to see the children. I wasn't happy. I knew he would try to win them over by spoiling them and taking them to places I couldn't afford. I mentioned this to Carlos, and I couldn't stop the tears. I knew Crystal loved her dad and Marsha wasn't bothered. The thought of a wedge being created between my two children troubled me. Remembering my mother's words from a few days ago when we all visited. "A broken home can have an effect on the children." Carlos knew Gary would want to see them and that was fine. Although I felt a sense of insecurity. One night as we were alone, I asked him, "How do you really feel about Gary coming to the house?"

His response was brief and swift. "He is their father, and that's only right." He never spoke about this again.

The first day when Gary rang the bell. I thought, *he's outside the door*. I felt anxious and sick. My legs felt weak and light. A feeling of apprehension washed over me; I didn't know what to expect. I didn't really want to see him or for him to take my girls. I put food on the table; I worked my ass off to look after them. He didn't deserve to see them. Did he do this to get back at me? Was he using the children? What was his real agenda? He didn't take them anywhere. This man didn't take them to the park. That was a chore for him. I really didn't want to look at him. I opened the door slightly. I was angry. He constantly hit me. I looked at him closely for the first time. I saw a person who appeared to be quiet and in control, but fidgety. He didn't look my way but I knew he was watching me from the corner of his eye.

He looked like he had just come from church. He looked smart in his suit. His voice was soft and came across as calm. I noticed he would clear his throat, which he used to do if he was nervous. He gave no eye contact. As I glanced at him, I sensed he didn't know what to say. Crystal came out happy and smiling. Marsha came out with a frown on her face and said nothing. Her two middle fingers in her mouth. Marsha said, "I want to stay with you, Mummy."

"You'll be back at 6pm, Marsha. Your dad wants to spend time with you."

When Gary came for the girls, we had nothing to discuss unless it was about the children.

As the weeks went by, I noticed Crystal was looking forward to seeing her dad. Marsha wasn't bothered and still didn't want to go with him. I got used to the girls being taken every two weeks by Gary. It meant Carlos and I had to plan our time together without the children. We continued going to church and enjoying our lives. Sometimes the girls would ask me to go to church with them and their dad. I sometimes thought about how Carlos felt, as he had been looking after the children for so long. It seemed Gary was now in our lives for some reason. I didn't bring it up as I sensed Carlos mentioned nothing about it. I didn't want to open up a bag of worms. I really cared for and loved Carlos for all he had done for us. He never changed; he always remained consistent. I had to accept that Gary was going to be a part of the girls' lives. I also had to get on with my life, with Carlos.

Gary collected the girls as usual every two weeks. As time went on, we spoke about the children. A year later he asked if I could speak to three members of his church. I agreed. When they arrived, they were two women and one man. The man had a black suit and black shoes, with a white shirt. The women had hats on. One had a black jacket and skirt, with a pink top and flat shoes. The other woman had a black jacket, skirt with a blue jumper and flat shoes. They appeared to be very nice. They smiled and began by introducing themselves. The man said, "Gary has asked us to come and speak to you regarding your marriage and the children. They explained that God allowed us to fall in love, to marry, and to have two children. He spoke about marriage being sacred and that we shouldn't marry again to another. He read how Gary should love me, as God loved the church and died for it. Gary started saying that he still loved me and wanted me back. He then asked if he could make a commitment. During the meeting, Gary gave his life to the Lord. I was overwhelmed. I really didn't think he would do this. They asked me if I had given my life to the Lord. The answer was 'Yes'. It was a shock for me to see Gary. do this because he never spoke about God at any time.

As time went by, he asked to take the children to church and invited me. I Carlos about it and he didn't disagree. I went to the service. It was very different from my church service. I came away thinking, has he really changed? Is he trying everything to get me back, but why? Was he making all this up? Was this the truth? Crystal loved her father.

The girls both cared and loved Carlos, too. I was very confused and couldn't imagine being without Carlos. This thought of disobeying God made me think about my daughters. I talked to Carlos about my thoughts. He told me that if I wanted to go back with Gary, he wouldn't stand in my way. As he is the father of the children. The next time Gary came to collect the girls, it was awkward. I didn't speak about anything with him. I had

Carlos' feelings to consider. He has been my rock through all my pain. He has helped me more than Gary has. I had a lot to think about. Carlos was very supportive as usual and didn't push or try to convince me to stay with him. All he told me; I had to decide myself. He understood the situation and wanted me to be happy.

After some time, Carlos and I began to drift apart. I know we didn't want to hurt each other. The girls were old enough to get ready for school by themselves. I left in the morning at 7am and finished at 4.30pm and got in soon after they came in from school. Carlos still visited but there was a change. Neither of us said anything. Gradually we stopped being close and became good friends. Then it went down to weekly, then it became longer until we had drifted apart. If we saw each other in the street, we would greet each other with a friendly hug and stand and talk.

13.
SECOND MARRIAGE

As time went on, Gary collected the children and took them out. We then were on speaking terms. We would laugh and have conversations regarding the girls or things in general. He started coming into the house and the children were thrilled to see us laughing and joking. It seemed like the old times when we were dating. He was very funny; his laugher was contagious. They say time is a healer. The past seemed like a distant memory that I didn't remember. I felt ok and went with it. I went to church with Gary and didn't visit my church as much. Before long, Gary asks me to marry him again and promised he would look after me and the children. I was overwhelmed. I asked the children, "What do you think about me and your dad got married again? They were over the moon. We both spoke about it as a family. It seemed like a fairy tale. I had to tell Carlos before anyone else did.

I went to his flat and told him. Carlos didn't look shocked or happy. He was very calm and said, "I hope everything goes well for you and the children." He showed no aggrievance at all. I left feeling better. I had told him face to face. I wanted to tell him first. I also invited him to the wedding. After a few months the date was arranged. Invitations were given out. My dress was being made by my cousin Pauline. We had two chief bridesmaids, my friend Ava, who fought for me in school. The other was Julie, a very good friend from my church. Both she and her husband John supported me throughout. The caterers were chosen from Gary's church. The wedding reception was at another church. I think we wanted it to be neutral. It all felt like a fairytale story. Everyone was happy for us and felt it was a great blessing. Ruthy, Sandra, and my father were not happy at all. They told me I was doing the wrong thing and that I would regret it. Ruthy and Sandra still insisted on dressing me at their home. They both loved me as their daughter and wanted me to look beautiful. (I was overwhelmed by the love they showed me even though they didn't agree with my decision}.

I was dedicated to God and His promises. I felt we could tell the mountains to move and they would have to move, as long as God was in the midst of everything in our lives. I wore a beautiful white dress with a trail made of lace and a matching hat that fitted my head perfectly, leaving some of my curly hair out. I felt beautiful and pleased with the handy work of my cousin Pauline, who made the outfit. My Pastor David. was giving me away. My father couldn't because of his legs, which weren't too well. I also felt that my father was against this wedding, like some other family members who came. I felt very happy that everyone came together from the two churches to make our wedding very special, and the church brothers and sisters were hopeful and happy for us. The girls were the bridesmaids dressed in white, and Ava and Julie, who was a sister from my church. They dress were light blue and white that matched the two girl's dresses, which matched their flowers in their flower baskets. The church overflowed with people from two churches when we arrived. Walking down the aisle, I was jittery, feeling butterflies in my tummy. I felt so happy I couldn't smile enough. I was overwhelmed by the sound of the music, the claps, the voices of Amen from so many people that were praying for us and this day. I could have cried when Gary looked back as I walked up the aisle and smiled with a look of love and admiration. Arriving at the altar, my father figure, David, gave me away to Gary. We both looked at each other and smiled. It all felt like a dream. Everything was perfect. As we said our vows, it was so personal, the true meaning of what marriage is to God. Binding this agreement with rings that we exchanged with each other felt powerful. The importance of dedication and giving each other the love that is sacred unto God. This was a demand and not to be taken lightly.

The service was great. Then the pictures were taken in the church and in the green area of the church outside. There were lots of pictures being taken. The sun was shining; and the day was perfect. The girls enjoyed the attention and my mum was happy for us. My dad gave a smile and spoke to Gary's mother. Gary's dad was a man of few words. They were speaking friendly. I could see my mother looking and observing. There were mixed emotions going around as I looked at certain people who weren't sure about our marriage. We enjoyed every moment of this wedding ceremony. It was my dream to have a beautiful church wedding, especially as our first wedding was at the register office with only two friends as witnesses. After the pictures were taken, we were driven to the reception hall. When we got into the hall, it looked amazing. The tables had white tablecloths and vases with red and white roses placed in the middle.

It was time for the speeches. David, who gave me away, mentioned how long he had known me. He saw my growth in the Lord and how dedicated I was to my faith. He wishes us all the very best and hoped God will guide us and keep us in His mighty peace. Then, others came up to congratulate us on our special day.

After the speeches, Carlos came in and sat right in front of our table. As I sat there, I noticed he didn't give me any eye contact or acknowledge anyone at the top table. He spoke to the surrounding others. He ate, then he left. Then, Ruthy and Sandra came up to me. Ruthy told me, "We're not stopping, just wanted to say hello. So, I'll see you, ok?"

"Yes, Ruthy." I replied, and they waved and disappeared. I thought I will not think about this now. I will think about it later. On the evening of the wedding, my Mum had a get together for family and friends. The children were staying with her for a few days. I passed around to see everyone. There was a full-on party going on. Everyone was happy and enjoying themselves. I didn't stay long as we were going on a short break, a honeymoon, which was a surprise from the members of my church.

We enjoyed the break and each other's company in Spain. Stepping off the plane, we encountered scorching temperatures. It gloriously recalled the West Indies. Such beautiful scenery. All the building was white. The hotel was very nice. As we arrived, the staff were very welcoming, with big smiles on their faces. We were shown our room, the dining lobby with colourful tablecloths. There were people already there enjoying their holiday. Our room was very spacious with a double bed, an enormous bathroom with a shower and a veranda where we sat and viewed the beautiful scenery. It was a beautiful day. The sun was blistering with a lovely warm breeze that helped to cool me down and feeling the blazing sunlight on my face. It felt so wonderful.

It was different from being with Carlos. I then noticed Gary was very quiet at times. I was used to Carlos making jokes and it would be laughter, most of the time. I felt bad because I was thinking about Carlos and I wondered why.

After the honeymoon, I went to mum house to collect the children. They always had a good time there; they got what they wanted and loved their grandma so much. They were glad to see me and asked for their father. "Dad is at home; you'll see him soon." I told them, "Mum, how was the party?"

"Oh, Ronnie, everyone enjoyed themselves. It didn't finish until late, around 4am. How was your break?"

"It was very nice, Mama. We had a good rest and the hotel was nice. It was so good of the church to pay for our break; now, I'm exhausted. Thanks for having that party and looking after the girls for me. I don't know what I would do without you. I really mean that, Mama. I have to make tracks; these girls have to go to bed for school tomorrow. I will see you on Friday. Please take care Mama. I'm working, but if you ever need anything, please let me know, Mama, I mean it."

'Ok, Ronnie."

It was very nice to see the girls coming home to see their dad. They hugged him and he hugged them. As I watch from a distance, I felt happy we were all together again. The next day, we had breakfast and the girls came into our bedroom and into the bed with us. It was a special time for them. Gary read from the bible and I prayed and the girls prayed one after the other. We were a family again.

At this time, Gary didn't have a job, but he was looking for work. I was still at the engineering company. Prior to getting married to Gary. I told him I was buying the house. Finally, the papers came and I had to sign for the house, which was now mine. It was difficult as he wasn't working, but we were married again. I just felt it was only right for him to sign for the house, too. At that moment it felt like a good gesture but as I thought about it, I questioned myself. I decided to buy my house. Gary came in on time just to sign his name on the dotted line. I used the money I got as compensation for the accident a few years back for a deposit on the house. We were happy for a while. As time went by, he eventually got a job at a company that distributed kitchen furniture. Gary told me he isolated himself and read the Bible at break and lunch times. Work colleagues spoke to him only if they had to. At home he was very quiet, irritable and detached himself from the children and me. This was a very hard time for us all, as before this, the house was always full of laughter, jokes, and happiness.

Three years into this marriage, and the children, who were now aged nine and six, noticed and asked, "What's up with dad?"

I said, "He's not feeling well today." I felt I had to be very careful. I didn't want the children to become worried or anxious. I was very careful not to keep them around him for too long. This became a normal pattern. I tried to be supportive, showing that I was there if he needed to talk. We could go out for a meal? He didn't want to do that either. Whatever I said wasn't good enough, or he accuse me of over-exaggerating.

What my dad, Ruth, and Sandra said came back to bite me in the bum. I then watched his moods and his actions towards the children. He didn't help with the cleaning or cooking when he came home. I went into the kitchen and cooked whilst he watched TV. One day I approached him and said, "Hi Gary, help me cook today?"

"I'm tired. I'll help you tomorrow." The next day he did the same thing, watched the TV and expected me to work, cook and look after the children. He refused to do anything but watch TV. One day I got the children ready and told them, "We are going out for something to eat." I then told him I would not be cooking tonight, as I was taking the girls out to eat.

The first thing he said was, "What about me?"

I said, "What about you? You cook something for yourself."

He looked at me with piercing eyes, raised brows, and a frown on his face. "So, this is what you're going on with, ok." and turned his head and continued watching the TV.

After coming back from the Chinese restaurant, the girls were happy and contented that I had taken them out. Gary was still watching TV with a screwed-up ball of paper on the floor next to him that suggested he had gone out and got fish and chips. He didn't look my way and I just glanced at him. The girls were washed, dressed, said their prayers, and went to bed. I got showered, went to bed, and fell asleep. Later that night. Gary entered the bedroom and got into bed. We turned our backs on each other that night.

The next day, as usual, I got up. I was the first to leave the house at 7.15am. Gary got up for work and would leave for 8.15am. The girls would leave the house at 8.30am for school. When I got home, Gary was in the kitchen cooking. He wasn't very good at it. I helped him and we were ok again. After that, he slipped back, and I reminded him I would not be doing all the cooking, cleaning, and looking after the children. As time went by, he was still working at the same place. I was still at the engineering company. He would wash up and do things around the house. We just got on with life. We agreed to have a third child and shortly after making this decision; I became pregnant with our 3rd child. Crystal was now 12, and Marsha was nine. When we told the girls I was having a baby, they were over the moon. I worked until I could receive statutory maternity pay. I was glad, as I was very unwell. I had to be on bed rest for most of the time. Gary was supportive and tried to help me as best as he could. My Mum rallied around. He had to cook, clean, and the girls contributed by doing their chores. My pregnancy was very painful and I couldn't do much. I spent most of the time feeling sick and laying down.

Shortly after, I was about a few weeks earlier than usual. I had Sabrina two weeks after Christmas.

I was admitted to hospital. I was told I would have to get a Caesarean Section (C.S) which was best for the baby and myself. Gary could be with me through the procedure. Baby Sabrina was born. She had brown eyes, a cute little nose and a light brown complexion and a round little face. She was perfect and looked more like Marsha when she was born. Crystal had a dark brown skin colour, like her father. Baby Sabrina was silent. All I wanted was for her to be ok, which she was. I had to stay in the hospital for several days because of my having a C-section. My mother and Gary looked after the girls until I came out of hospital. Coming home was great. I missed home and the girls. It seemed that they had grown more, especially Crystal. "Wow, I said to Crystal, you have shot up since I have been in the hospital!". She started laughing. I pulled her and Marcha towards me and gave them big hugs and kisses for being good girls for Mum and Dad.

The next day my friends came to see baby Sabrina and me. One of my friends, Pricella was a midwife and helped me with feeding baby Sabrina, because she wouldn't latch on to the breast. I met her when I joined Gary's church; we became very good friends. She had hair short and curly; she wore glasses and was always smiling. Her laughter was contagious. I really appreciated her kindness and patience. We would pray together. I could tell her anything. She spoke with wisdom and helped me when I needed the support. Another friend who was very understanding was Violet. She was very shy and quiet. As she got to know me, we also became good friends and again we prayed and read the Bible together. They both became friends that were very trustworthy. Gary noticed but never mentioned it.

When baby Sabrina was six weeks old, I saw Carlos at the shop. He knew I had a baby and said he would like to see her and the girls. I said he could. We agreed on a date and a time, which was in two weeks on a Sunday. We would go to his flat and he would cook for us. I told Gary and he said that was Ok. Crystal, Marsha, baby Sabrina and I went. It was great seeing Carlos. The girls were thrilled to see him, and so was I.

I then observed Gary and I were silent more than we conversed. He lost his job. He didn't look for another and he became complacent. There were five of them in a group in the church. He was very focused, praying and depending on being famous or well known. Unfortunately, it didn't happen. They song at different churches but eventually they split up. This was the beginning of Gary becoming depressed and gave up on working and supporting anyone in the family. It was very hard to see and be around it. He was in a group at church and had all his focus on being famous; the group didn't work out, and it seems all his hopes and dreams went down the drain. He would sit there staring at the TV. He became very aggressive and wouldn't do anything in the house.

I felt my world was falling apart. My father wasn't well. I had to get my mum a flat as soon as possible. At this time, my father was becoming more violent and I had to get my mother out of the house they were living in. I had to get flat for mum to stay so she would be safe. My house was too small and I had a man who didn't want to work and who was depressed. I couldn't bring my mother into the atmosphere and into this mess. After telling the doctor and housing and Citizens Advice Bureau, getting a flat was very urgent. A flat became mine immediately because it was an emergency. I couldn't sleep or eat very well. I was worried and frightened about my mother's safety. I moved her out whilst my dad was not in. I arranged a van, the girls, and Charles, a family friend. He was very tall and was not frightened of my father; he was also very strong and could try to calm my father down, if it came to it. We were all females. I needed a backup plan and reassurance to give us a hand. I knew if my father got back before, it wouldn't have been good. I prayed the night before and prayed throughout the incident.

I went to the council to have her moved into a flat. This was a very sad time for Mum but she knew Dad was not himself. I also had to monitor dad also because of his condition. He has always been a man who wasn't bothered about saying what he felt about anyone. I knew he had changed; later, doctors diagnosed him with dementia. There was a flat next door to Mum. I felt even though they couldn't live together. They still could visit each other. Also, I could keep an eye on them both. I arranged home care.

I arranged for them to receive three daily visits from home care workers. In the morning, the workers washed them and provided breakfast. They were given their lunches around 12- 1pm and washed and changed for bed around 7.30 to 8.00pm in the evening. Having care in place allowed me not to worry about my parents whilst I was working. I would phone them during the day and visit them both after work.

    I was still doing my hairdressing at home with a few clients after having baby Sabrina. A good friend of my mother's, Miss Evie, told me about Lexi, who wanted someone to manage her shop before and after her child was born. This person contacted me and we arranged an interview. The job was managing her business, whilst she gave birth until she was able to return to work. I prayed about this job and decided to accept it, and decided if it suited me, I wouldn't go back to the engineering company. Gary was at home, so he could look after baby Sabrina until a nursery place came up, which would be in a few weeks. The girls were old enough to get themselves' home and look after baby Sabrina. If their dad needed to go anywhere. Crystal was 16 and had a part-time job in the evenings. She went straight from school and returned home around 7pm. Marsha was 13 and came straight home after school. She could watch baby Sabrina until he came back.

    The salon's colours were green and white. Lexi greeted me and took me to the back so we could speak. There were a lot of products on standing units with shelves displayed for clients as soon as you entered the shop. The reception area was on the right-hand side as you came into the shop. There was a room at the back. There were two fitted dressing stations with two chairs, and two mirrors on the wall. On the back wall, there were two wash basins.

    Lexi had a light brown complexion, with a broad smile, with full makeup and bright red lips, with extensions to her shoulders; Lexi was heavily pregnant, wearing a green suit and a white blouse. She spoke with a London accent and came across as very confident; she needed a trustworthy person whom she could rely on to run her business. I listened closely to her requirements and needs and what she expected from me. She told me that a friend had recommended me to her. She wanted someone to work for her until she returned to work and to continue working if it suited me. I then showed her my certificates and then she asked me if I would be interested in having the position. She explained what the position entailed. I would be completely responsible for the takings for the shop each day. At the end of each week, she would like me to go to her house with the taking's records. She also wanted to know our client count, the treatments I offered, and the products sold. Then she would give me my wages. She needed me to start in two weeks.

I accepted the position. We arranged another appointment to show me how to work the alarm, how to close the shutters and where could I leave the takings as I didn't want to have them on my person. Where to order products if I ran out. We decided on the date and time of the next meeting. We met a few days later to discuss my wages, the code to get into the shop, shutters, etc. I felt happy with our agreement.

The two weeks soon passed and I was opening up the salon. I bought two uniforms. One was white and the other was black. When anyone came into the salon, I would use my skills to ensure they felt welcomed. The word got around. I gradually had a good clientele base, as people were advertising the salon and acknowledging my work. It was difficult at times, as I had to stick to appointments only. I went to Lexi's home, as agreed. She was over the moon about the takings. It continued until she came back to the salon. She was not pleased, as clients would bypass her at reception and acknowledge me. I felt she became very envious of the treatment I was getting from clients and she wasn't impressed.

One of her friends visited the salon daily. They had long conversations and laughed constantly. I recognised his face but didn't know him by name. Lexi was overwhelmed by the number of clients that came into the salon. She told me she wanted to expand the business. I said nothing because I wouldn't be involved. I realised I could run my own salon. I was thanking God for the opportunity to look after someone else's business. I learnt so much from the experience of running the salon. I was grateful to Lexi for the opportunity. I then noticed the changes in her. She wasn't friendly as before. I continued working. Observing Lexi's actions, she would gaze at me but hardly gave me eye contact. Suddenly, she started speaking down to me. I know I ran her business right; takings doubled after I started working for her. *Did she have another agenda?* I made sure I smiled and greeted her as usual when I arrived every morning. Her friend came in as usual every day. They would talk and laugh loudly, even if there were clients in the salon. Clients would look at me as they sensed there was something wrong. Lexi employed a beautician. The beautician's name was Paulette. She was Asian, aged 25. She didn't smile or give me much eye contact but greeted everyone as they came through the door. She was very reserved and didn't speak very much. She only spoke if she needed information. I tried to ignore everything that was going on around me. I noticed an estate agent came. He and Lexi disappeared, possibly to view the building next door. On their return, I heard Lexi say, "I will get in touch very soon," and he left. I felt Lexi was trying to make me feel uncomfortable and I didn't know why. Shortly after, on a Saturday evening, Lexi told me she was letting me go tonight. This was what I told her that my friend did to me. Now she was doing the same thing. I said, "Ok that's fine, but I need my wages?"

She said, "I will give you your wages on Monday."

"Why can't you give me my wages now?" I wanted to cry, because I was so shocked and couldn't believe that I had told her Emma did that and now, she was doing the same thing. I had just finished my last client. A voice came from within me and told me, "Say nothing."

I made sure I washed everything, basins, mirrors, and floors. I left that evening without my wages. I prayed to God to carry me through this moment. I was relying on my wages to feed my children, myself and Gary. I went and told my mother what had happened. My mum said, "Don't worry Ronnie, God sees all things. I will give you some money for some groceries. Don't worry, darling." My mother gave me £40 to buy some shopping. I had nothing that night to feed my children, Gary and myself. I thanked my Mum, and told her, "I don't know what would happen if you weren't here for me, Mum."

I went to the shop and bought groceries for dinner and for another two days. *I will always look after my Mum. She is my saviour, in more ways than one.* When I got home, I told Gary what happened. He couldn't believe that she was so brutal and inconsiderate towards me. I told him I went down to Mum, and she kindly gave me £40 for tonight, Sunday, and Monday's dinner. He said, "That's kind of your Mum." (Gary couldn't help me, which was shameful and ridiculous. I wondered if he felt any shame at all.) Again, I praised my mother because I don't know how I would've survived without her. God bless her for all she does for me and mine. I was very upset that Lexi didn't give me my wages.

On Monday around 12noon, I went up to the salon for my wages. I got my car out of the garage at the back of the house. When I arrived at the salon, Paulette told me that Lexi had just left and had gone to my house to give me my wages. I then thought, *this is not a coincidence*. Lexi left my wages with Gary in a sealed envelope. When I got it. I prayed over it for God to bless it and sanctify it.

I was now without a job. How would I pay for my mortgage, bills, and food? I left everything in the mighty name of Jesus and believed that I was the apple of God's eye and He would carry me through all things. I had to trust and believe. Meantime, what will I do for an income? Gary wasn't working.

I then heard of a driving job, taking children to school and back. I went to the person who was in charge and she gave me a job. I was given a list of the names of the support assistant and the child I would pick up. I started at 7.45am. The children had learning difficulties. Some of them couldn't talk but made noises when they were trying to talk or show you something. It was very hard to see. There were no words to express what I felt for them. I did this job for six months. I was still working at home with clients. I would fit them in around this job.

Driving past Lexi's shop, which was on the main road. I realised it had been empty for some time. I went to the business centre that was overseeing all the units. I felt something inside telling me to enquire about the shop. Going into the business centre, I asked the receptionist what I should do if I was interested in the unit. She advised me to put my name down and the manager would contact me in due course. I then put my name down and left.

The shop was close to where I lived. I would drive past every day to see if it was still closed. One day I saw a notice on the window stating, NO ONE IS ALLOWED TO ENTER THIS BUILDING UNLESS GIVEN PERMISSION. I then went into the business centre again and asked the receptionist if the unit was now vacant. She told me they had given the unit to someone. I then explained that I had put my name down four months ago. She looked in the book and asked me my name and it was another name. She then rang the Manager at my request.

The manager asked if I would like to come upstairs to discuss this issue. I knocked, and a voice loudly said, "Come in!" I went into this room. The manager stood up and greeted me with a handshake. He had dark skin, was very tall and wore glasses. He seemed very pleasant, with a friendly smile. "What can I do for you, sorry what is your name?"

"My name is Veronica Liburd. I am here regarding the unit next door. I understand the unit has been vacant for some time. I realise the former owner has left. I came to the business centre and put my name down. I learned someone else had already been given the unit when I enquired. When I came in four months ago, no one had put their names down. I saw the unit was closed, with a notice saying that no one should enter this property without permission."

I could see that he looked worried. "Ok, I will look into this and get back to you. We have your details. We will get back to you as soon as possible."

"Thanks, looking forward to hearing from you," I said as I left.

I later learned that they gave the unit to someone in another county. The unit had to be given to someone who lived in the area.

*****

Three Months Prior

The manager called me into the office to speak about the unit. He apologised for the mistake that had been made and said the unit was mine if I still wanted it. I was so excited. He asked me if I wanted the furniture that was left. I knew I could refurbish the furniture. I agreed on the price of the furniture, the cost of the unit and the rates. He took me into the salon. It was so weird walking into this space again, but this time it was mine. I could feel my stomach turning. A joy that I couldn't stop as I wanted to scream and dance for joy. I couldn't stop smiling. I just didn't want this feeling to stop. I felt like a child who had a full jar of every sweet I loved and hoped for. I just gave God the glory and the praise. I knew what colour I wanted for the shop, for the furniture and, above all, I had already got a name.

This came to mind; If you take care of someone else's treasure, you will eventually get your own treasure when the time comes. Again, I drove to Mama's flat and told her everything. She was so happy for me but said, "Oh Ronnie, I hope that woman will not do you anything because you have her shop."

"Oh, Mum, if God is for me, who can be against me? I didn't rush to go home. I had cooked for two days. When I eventually got home; I knew the girls would be in bed. I felt I needed this time with my Mum, and I wasn't bothered.

Gary wasn't happy. I could see he had a frown on his face. He looked at me from the corner of his eye. "Where have you been?"

"I went to see the manager at the business centre, and guess what... they offered me the shop, and all the furniture for a good price. What do you think?"

"Yes, that's good." I looked at him and I knew he wasn't really happy for me. I didn't care whether or not he liked it. *Tonight, I'm going to rejoice and be glad.* This is my time to be happy. The next weeks were tough, as I knew Gary was very quiet, not speaking. I would try to involve him in conversations but he would nod his head or just keep looking straight ahead at the television. I sometimes wondered, *what is he really thinking? I hope he is not getting so depressed that he is losing his faculties.*

14

CHANGE HAS COME

It all changed when I became a businessperson and he felt I was leaving him behind. Everyone was now looking at my achievements and no one was looking at him. This was what he couldn't believe or accept. He asked me, "Why is the Lord answering your prayers and not mine?" After having three children with him.

Gary was very insecure and took his frustration out on me. He became very depressed and wouldn't find work. He really wanted to be a singer and when the group split up in the church that we attended, his dreams crumbled too. He started looking at my success. This was the beginning of our marital breakdown.

One morning, he wanted me to have sex with him. I told him, "No, I have to go to work." He got very upset and started roughing me up, dragging me from left to right and pulling my nighty up. "No, I don't want to!" I protested. He started slapping me and beating me. "Stop it!" I shouted. Then he took up a heavy full-length mirror, which was leaning by the wall, and lifted it up as if to smash it over my head. At this point, I reminded him that I was the mother of his children. Then suddenly the door flew open and in came Crystal and Marsha, who were 16 and 13. They told me to run. I was so frightened I ran out of the house with my nighty and nothing else on.

I was so fearful I asked my next-door neighbour to call the police but they refused. I was scared to go back into the house because I knew he would kill me. But I could hear my daughter's shouting. I was crying but scared. I saw Marsha run outside. She kept on running across the street, saying, "I'm going to get help! He's beating up Crystal!" I was too scared to go in and help my own daughter. After beating her, he violently dragged her down the stairs by her hair while she screamed for him to stop. The police came and as they took him out and handcuffed him, he was saying sorry to me. I just ignored him. I saw my youngest daughter, Sabrina, sitting on the step. "Oh, my baby!" and I started crying, hoping she didn't see any of this mess. The ambulance came and took my daughters and me to the hospital. I felt so ashamed; the whole neighbourhood knew what happened, and tongues were wagging.

I heard that the pastor of our church had to bail him out, and after that, he was not allowed to come near the house. He stayed with an old lady from the church and still continued to go to the church, but I refused to go. I had a visit from two brothers from the church. As we were talking, one of them said, "We can finish off the decorating for you if you want us to." I welcomed the help. They came after a few days and finished decorating the stairs and the hallway.

I didn't attend for months and didn't see Gary for quite a long time. One week, they had a special speaker at the church. I decided to go with Marsha and Sabrina. I didn't see him in the church. As I was driving home, I saw him. He had lost a lot of weight and he looked like the person I married all those years ago. Marsha and I looked at each other. Marsha asked, "Mummy, can we give him a lift?" I could see in her eyes she felt what I felt in my heart that evening. I stopped and offered him a lift.

This was the start of his coming back into our lives. After a few weeks I invited him back into the house. I mentioned this to Crystal but I knew she wouldn't be as forgiving as Marsha. After all, Crystal had suffered at the hands of her so-called father, who beat her up and put her in hospital and pulled hair out of her scalp. Crystal told me if he came back, she would leave and go and will live with my Mum.

It happened. He moved back in, and Crystal left. I didn't blame her at all. I prayed about the situation and asked God to help me have a healing relationship with my daughter. I had to have patience. Crystal lived with my mum for over one year. She loved living at her grandmother's house because grandmother gave her the space she needed. She would often retreat to her bedroom, saying, "Crystal, make sure you lock the door, before settling down to sleep.

At home, I felt trapped, going nowhere. He didn't cook, clean, or tidy the house. He did nothing but watch television all day. I was working most of the time only to come home to an untidy house full of dirty cups and dishes. He would ask me what we were eating tonight. I was bringing home the bacon. Whilst he felt the whole world was against him. 255 British lives were lost in the 74-day Falkland War—the first post-WWII conflict. His part-time Territorial Army service sparked war talk. He was very frightened when there was talk of signing people up. This added to his stress levels, and he took it out on me.

According to him, I was always working and hardly cooking; he said I didn't give him anytime and the girls were becoming a problem. The more he was negative, the more I became driven, ambitious, and motivated. This was my only survival mechanism. Foremost, came God, my Creator, my mother, my girls, and my business.

After a while, I noticed traits in his behaviour and felt I had to monitor his moods. I would not stay whilst he carried on with Marsha and me. He started hitting Marsha a lot, whilst I was not around.

One day a friend of the family told me, while I was at the shop, he saw Marsha walking the streets with no shoes. I finished with my client and went home quickly, only to witness broken glass and he was sitting there very upset and all flustered with Sabrina on his lap. I was full of hurt, disgusted and very upset that Sabrina would have seen and heard all of this commotion and witnessed him hitting Marsha. Now I have to find my poor broken child, who is wandering around the streets. I asked, "Where is Marsha?"

He replied, "I don't know where she is."

"What happened?" I asked him.

He replied, "She's answering me back. She wouldn't do what I asked her to do, so I slapped her, then she walked out of the house." I went out in the car looking for Marsha but I didn't find her. Later on, Marsha came back. I noticed he had a lot of mood swings and was depressed about everything. The memory of him beating us up sent shivers down my spine; if it happened again, we might not survive. I could feel his anger and frustration when he spoke to me.

He was working as a home help assistant in the neighbourhood. He would bring things up that weren't all that important and make them into something huge. I was very aware of his moods. He would try to wind me up to argue with him. He got so angry because I didn't answer him; he took the hoover and threw it over the banister. He didn't even look to see where it landed. He ran downstairs, then went out the door and slammed it.

Looking out of the window as he walked across the street. I phoned my 2nd sister, Ester, and told her what had happened and that I was going into a hostel. I had gone to the office previously and reported my concerns, so I had to wait a few days for a vacancy. They rang me and told me there was a vacancy now for us. I was just praying and waiting.

Mum and Dad

Me Aged 8 or 9

My Niece, Cousin and I

My Hair Dressing Graduation with Mama

My Best Friend

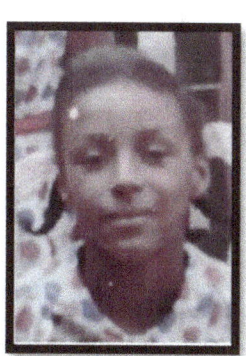

My First Salon

Me and My Carlos

Me and My Girls I was about 29

My Girls

Mama and my aunts in the West Indies

Our Family Trip to the West Indies

My daughters and Granddaughter and Me with Mama

My Grandchildren

15.
WAKE-UP CALL

There was a young woman who came to the salon regularly. She dressed smartly and was very pleasant. We used to speak a lot. I knew she had trouble with her boyfriend; she mentioned it. Two weeks later he chased her down the road and killed her by chopping her head off. This woke me up. It made me so aware of what can go on in people's heads. The whole community was in shock. He looked very quiet, smartly dressed and appeared pleasant.

I needed to go now. I started praying as I packed the bags into the car. He was nowhere in sight. I collected my youngest daughter from nursery and went to my Mum to tell her I was moving. "Mum, I'm going into a hostel, and don't mention anything to him. I feel ok because Crystal is here with you, Mum. I feel that my heart is jumping out of my chest, Mum". I was so frightened and can't believe what I have to do. Mum, my mind is working overtime now. I will let you know how I get on. Just please keep praying for me. Love you, Mum. I'm going now, Mum." And I kissed and hugged her goodbye.

"I'm going to collect Marsha from school," I informed the headmaster. "It's an emergency." I rang up the hostel to let them know we were coming. I prayed Gary would suspect nothing. I began checking in my head for anything I should have for the business, all my bank books, cards, mortgage documents, which I had sorted previously. I had all of our clothes. *Well, God, I'm putting everything in your hands now.*

My business was in the area where the house was. I had to be very vigilant and careful when leaving the shop now.

When we got to the hostel. I rang the bell. A voice replied, "Can I help you?"

"My name is Veronica. I was told to come in." I entered the building, not knowing what to expect. I was greeted by Alice, an assistant.

She asked, "have you got any belongings with you?"

"Yes, I have clothes, quite a lot, actually."

"That's not a problem. Did you come by transport?"

"Yes, I have a car. Is it ok to park outside?"

"Yes, but if you wish, you can park in our car park. It's at the back of the building."

"Yes, that would be great. I will take the clothes out of the car, then park it at the back."

"Yes, that's ok." Alice took us upstairs in the lift. We walked almost to the end of the corridor.

She stopped at number 45 and unlocked the door. Walking into the flat on the lefthand side was the kitchen area. It had a cooker. A small work top, with a kettle, microwave, and toaster on it. There was a sink, a small fridge. There was a small table with three chairs. On the right-hand side near the wall was a bunk bed and one bed. There was a door that led to the bathroom. It had a bath with a shower, a basin, and a toilet.

We carried the bags into the room. "Well, we are safe here. As long as we have a roof over our heads, I'm thankful." I was so tired; I gave the girls the food I bought earlier and took a bite for myself. Despite my tiredness, I needed to sharpen my thoughts. Anticipating how my life will turn out now.

The girls had a shower after eating, and they went to bed. My mind was full. *I'm in a hostel; this is so embarrassing. I'm never ever going back to him.* I sat in this small room. I felt closed in. I had to tell myself *This is not forever.*

I had to stay positive for the children. I felt upset, unloved, used, and abused. I found it difficult to sleep. I woke up the next morning way ahead of Marsha and Sabrina.

Marsha she couldn't get over the size of the space. "It looks like we are homeless, Mum."

"I know, but we will get through this. God will not let us down. He will make a way where there is no way. Let us pray. *Merciful Father, we are trusting you for all you give us and everything we have, at, this moment, it feels like we are on our own. Allow us to always depend on you for everything. Protect us and guard us as we leave everything in your hands in Jesus' name. Amen.*" Sabrina awoke soon after we prayed.

"I'm very anxious about going to the shop today, Marsha. I will have to be very careful. You will have to meet me at the shop. I will finish early today because I will have to pick up Sabrina from nursery. I have told the nursery Gary can't pick her up, only me from now. If you see your dad, don't tell him where we are."

"Yes, Mum, I understand."

At the nursery, there was no sign of Gary. I was happy about that. I drove Marsha to school. I opened up the shop. I then phoned my solicitor to tell her what had happened. I was reassured that she would write to Gary to let him know he can't come near me or the children. The letter would reach him today. I was relieved, as the shop was a few streets from the house. I kept the door locked and opened it only to let clients in and out. I asked anyone who was going to the shop for anything to buy me what I needed and they were happy to oblige. The day went quickly and I was finishing off my last client and Marsha came from school. I was glad she was ok. After the last client left, Marsha helped with the mopping, cleaning and tidying of the salon. Soon after, I locked up, shutters down and we were off. I looked around to see if there was any sign of Gary. I then drove off.

Arriving at the nursery, I was eager to know if he had tried to pick up Sabrina. I was told he didn't call or come down to the nursery, either. I was very anxious within my body and took a deep breath of relief. He was sometimes very unpredictable. We were very vigilant and careful that we weren't followed.

When we got to the hostel, I noticed there were some people on the same floor as us. Their door was opened as we passed. One of the boys came out of the flat to see what number we were in. I had a very suspicious feeling about this. I let Sabrina and Marsha in first, then I went in behind them. Then I glanced at the boy, who was staring. Afterwards, I thought nothing about it. The next day was the same routine, going to see Mum, giving her an update of what's happening, without worrying her too much. Also, we passed by to see Daddy.

Whilst Crystal was listening, she rolled her eyes and said, "I knew he would do it again." as she shook her head from side to side.

I listened and said, "I know Crystal. I know you told me, darling, you did." I felt like I was the child and my daughter was the adult. I stayed quiet. Crystal and Marsha went into the bedroom to speak after hearing what my daughter said.

"Mum, Gary hasn't been here, has he?"

"No, and I hope he doesn't." said mum.

Crystal shouted from the bedroom, "He better not!"

I told Mum and Crystal we had to go and told Mum I would come back tomorrow. I kissed and hugged Mum and told her how much I loved her. As Crystal and Marsha came out of the bedroom, they kissed and hugged each other. I kissed and hugged Crystal and told her, "I love you, darling."

I then went to see Dad; he seemed his usual self, very quiet, smoking his pipe, sitting and watching TV. I asked him, "How are you, Dad? Have you eaten?"

"Yes, they come and make me something to eat." Dad wasn't so talkative as usual, but I could see he wasn't himself.

"I came to see how you are, Dad. I have just come from work, so I will come and see you another time, ok?"

"Ok." he said.

"Goodbye, Dad, I'll see you soon. He didn't answer. I locked the door and threw the key back through the letterbox. Then we left. We picked

Sabrina up from nursery, our eyes constantly scanning for anyone who might be following.

Crystal soon got a flat and moved out. I knew Mum missed her but Crystal would still visit and stay with Mum one or two days a week until she got used to being on her own again. We were at the hostel for six weeks. I felt we had to get out. One evening, getting back to the hostel, there was a dreadful smell as we entered the corridor. It smelt stronger. As we approached our flat, we could see that there were faeces outside the door. I went back downstairs and told the person on duty and they came upstairs and witnessed it. It was bad and smelled throughout the corridors. I told Marsha and Sabrina to go downstairs until I called them. I felt so sick. I wanted to vomit. I also joined the girls downstairs. They told us to wait in the office until the corridor aired out.

Could it have been one of those blonde-haired boys, with faces of disapproval and disgust at being forced to live near people of dark skin? Someone came and cleaned up the faeces that stunk up the entire hallway. However, I didn't feel our belongings, or us, were safe.

I told Mum about the incident that occurred. My mother didn't hesitate and said, "You can stay here until you sort out the house."

I said, "Are you sure, Mum?"

"Yes, Ron." I didn't think about moving into Mum's one-bedroom flat at all.

I said, "Yes, Mum, I would be grateful if we could." I then told the manager at the hostel that we had somewhere to go and that we would move out tomorrow. On Wednesdays, the shop was closed. I didn't take Sabrina to nursery and Marsha didn't go to school. We moved into my mum's flat that day. Even though it was a one-bedroom flat, it was home. It was a relief to be with Mum, and not in the hostel. I contacted my solicitor to notify her of my decision about us moving in with Mum. She informed me that this would speed up the process of getting him out of the house. Living at mum's was good. I felt safer and it allowed me to see Mum and Dad every day. Mum was very happy for the company. It was more convenient for all of us.

Sabrina's nursery was at the bottom of the street. Marsha got a bus to school; also, the shop was close. Marsha would collect Sabrina from nursery and I could continue work and join them when my work was done. We soon got into a routine, and Mum and Dad saw me each day. My dad became worse, and I had to keep a closer eye on him. I would also visit Crystal at her flat to make sure she was ok. I felt I had a clearer mind and focused on moving forward.

At the shop, I was very busy. Before the incident at home, Crystal, and Marsha were helping in the shop on Saturdays. After the incident happened, Crystal didn't come back to the salon. I asked her if she would come back to work; she welcomed the offer; she had her flat now. I was over the moon to have my daughters working for me again. Sabrina was with my mother on Saturdays.

I didn't have any pressure from Gary; he had to stay away from us, according to my solicitor's instructions. Within three months we were able to move back into the house. It was sad to leave Mum, as she'd got used to us being there. She understood and knew she could stay with me at any time.

On our return, the house felt empty, not just the feelings but it was really empty. Again, Gary had stripped the house. He had taken the table and chairs, fridge/freezer, bed, carpets, cutlery, plates, beddings, and Sabrina's cot and pushchair. He was so predictable. I knew he would do this. No thought for his children, as usual. I was so glad to be back and make it our home again. Looking around the house brought back memories of the dark place I had been in.

There were times within my first marriage I became so depressed. Gary treated me with no respect. He would just sit on the floor and watch TV all day. He expected that everything to be done for him. I really resented him. He was always eating. Feeding himself with nuts, sweets, anything he could get his hands on.

I carried the whole family. I carried the responsibility for all of us. He would just shut off from reality. Oh, but he wanted us to make love each night! According to him, I hated every minute of it. I felt like I was just an object and he was my master. I was obliged to be used and abused as he needed. I was his wife and he could do anything he wanted and I had to agree. He was right. I hated every minute of it. There was no love in this. This was abuse. I remember him telling me he saw a rat in the kitchen, (this always reminded me of that UB40 song. *A rat in the kitchen. What are you going to do?*) he didn't even take responsibility for getting rid of the rat! I had to get a neighbour to help me.

Once the rat was removed, I had to stay in the kitchen and continue to scrub the cupboards, mop the floors, sterilise and wash all utensils, plates, and pots. I struggled to put them all on top of the cupboards, then cook. He left me to it and was adamant he wasn't going back into the kitchen and still wouldn't help me. The children had to eat; I couldn't afford takeaways every day. My neighbour assured me the rat would go back out the way it came in. The only place was the drain outside that was from the sewage. I had to call the water company. They treated it as an emergency and came out to fix the burst pipe. I gave God thanks. Lord, you've done it again.

During another dark period, I contemplated suicide by taking many paracetamol tablets. I felt everything was closing in on me. I thought of how Gary was so unkind and selfish. At the time, I felt trapped and couldn't find my way out of this life. I was looking at the box of tablets, thinking *I will take it*. Then the thought of my children came into my head. At that moment, the doorbell rang. I answered the door to see Jehovah's Witnesses standing there. I invited them in. They spoke about God and the kingdom. I felt rather guilty as I thought about what I had planned to do. I expressed my thoughts. "I'm so unhappy and unloved. My husband is always miserable and sad. He's no longer the man I fell in love with. He makes me feel like I'm not good enough. I just feel like ending it all." They told me anyone who kills themselves will not see God's face, because there is no repentance in the grave. That person will not enter the kingdom of God.

They told me if I wanted to go to Kingdom Hall on Sunday; I was welcome. I went to see how they worshipped. It was very different from the Church of England that I was used to. I went a few times, which I enjoyed. The whole congregation listened to the Jehovah's Witnesses'

Bible. (I couldn't get my head around their having their own bible.) I was grateful to God for sending them to me on that day.

Returning to this house, which had so many sad memories, was bittersweet. The house felt empty and unlived in. Gary left it in a mess. I just closed my eyes and thought, *I have been here before, but this will be the last time.* I decided I would not be speaking to Gary again. The person who I would definitely speak to was his youngest sister. She worked for me for several months to gain experience whilst she was at college. She was very nice; she didn't pick sides, but I knew our friendship may change. She had to leave eventually because of the situation. I told her, "I have always loved you, even though things haven't worked out between your brother and me. There will always be a soft spot in my heart for you. I love you, Julia. I will never stop speaking to you." We hugged and she left the salon.

I had to analyse my life. To move forward the best way I could. Lord, please help me move forward in your strength, because I am weak but you are strong. I continued to remind myself I'm never alone. As long as I have Jesus on the inside, that's all I need.

I suddenly felt lost and thought, *why did I ever marry him again?* I have heard this said, "A leopard never changes its spots." Now I knew what that meant.

Things needed to be done. I started in the kitchen, put on gloves and bleached the sink. Then continued washing the plates, cutlery, cups, and pots that he'd left dirty. Then I cleaned the cooker, the kitchen surfaces, and then swept and mopped the whole kitchen. I told Marsha to help with the hoovering. We worked throughout the house until everything was spotless. It took us most of the day. It was all done. The house smelt fresh and clean. Then I got us some takeaway to eat. This was our treat for our hard work. I would have to get a fridge/freezer to replace what he had taken.

I stopped going to the church. I noticed the attitude of some members. They pretended they didn't see me. I just stopped speaking to most of them. I wasn't prepared to play games. I felt that whatever happened, God knew and I prayed for guidance and wisdom. The salon became very popular. I had a great clientele. The business was very successful. I saw Gary. a few times but I didn't give him any eye contact. There was no communication regarding him seeing Sabrina. I knew his mind was set on other things.

At this time, Marsha left home and had her own flat. She also worked at the salon part time with Crystal. It was delightful to have my two daughters working in the business. Mama would have Sabrina from Friday until Sunday. This freed me up to be myself.

16.
Work Hard Play Hard

The salon was very busy. Clients were booking appointments. We were finishing very late each night, especially from Thursdays to Saturdays. On Saturdays, Crystal and Marsha would work and be paid. Mum used to have Sabrina from Friday until Sunday evening. This gave me the freedom to go out with friends and some of my clients. Allowing me to really enjoy myself and go to different venues, shows, and dances. These were the best times of my life and it never stopped me from praising and thanking my Heavenly Father for this time.

My mother would tell me, "Enjoy yourself, because you have gone through hard times. I'm here to watch over Sabrina, so enjoy yourself."

People would invite me to parties. I felt free for the first time in my life since the age of 18. I didn't have to worry about anyone. I could be me. It was freedom, joy, laughter. It was a time for me to be among people whose company I enjoyed. We danced, laughed and enjoyed ourselves. Most of the time, I would drive. I wouldn't drink whilst I was driving. If I did, which was very rare, I would leave the car and get a taxi home.

I would come home and stand in front of the mirror, dance and admire myself for a bit. Then, get ready for bed. This went on for a very long time. I enjoyed every minute of being single. I wasn't interested in anyone. I pushed aside my doubts, confident in God's control and direction. I started saving, being sensible, focusing on what was most important for the family. I recognised Mum wasn't as strong as she used to be. A thought came into my head: to take everyone to the West Indies for one month. I didn't tell anyone; I focused on the cost for everyone.

It took me one year to save up for our flights and spending money. Meanwhile, I knew a stylist who asked me if I needed anyone to work for a few days a week. After she worked for me, I felt her skills and attitude towards the clients was good. I knew it was a big risk to leave someone in charge of my business, but I felt I could trust her. After praying and getting over my anxiety, I asked her if she would look after the business for one month. She said, "Yes." and we agreed on her wages. I felt she was happy with the decision and put together a contract for her to sign.

I then told Mum, Crystal, Marsha, and Sabrina we were going to the West Indies. I don't think they believed me when I told them I had some money put aside for their clothes and they must start looking around. Mum didn't hesitate. Mum loved going to town. This was her main interest every week. Where she met friends and stopped to have big conversations with them. I loved watching them. They had it down to a tea. Bags down, and the whole world would stop. The place they stood was their space to talk about anything and everything.

When the girls realised I was really serious, there was an urgency to get their clothes, shoes, and bits and bobs together. I gave them the money to buy their clothes and other things. I haven't seen them so anxious and confused about what they wanted to wear and get. It was a joy to hear and see them so excited.

I had a niece working for me at this time. Looking back, If I could have changed things, I would have been more cautious and had her oversee everything. (My one regret, as she told me later, she would have done it). The business was busy with clients coming to get their hair done before I went on holiday. My niece wasn't a hairdresser but would have had my best interests at heart.

The time came quickly and before we knew it; we were on the coach going to the airport. At the airport, I got a wheelchair for Mum as I felt she wouldn't be able to stand for long.

I couldn't believe we were all going to the West Indies. All the family knew we were coming. The flight was calm and steady. We could have any drinks we wanted. I couldn't believe I had achieved this holiday by saving up and believing by faith we would get here. God, you've done it again. The flight was long; we slept most of the way. I felt blessed that I would see my Aunty Virginia again. I wonder if she was how I visualised her. I thought of the house, the big garden with trees full of fruit. Was it the way I remembered it in my mind? The only person I wouldn't see was my wonderful grandmother. I still miss her so much.

The islands welcomed us with brilliant sunshine. I had a feeling of freedom, excitement, and joy. I saw my mum's face with a smile and contentment. How amazing to look down at the Islands as we passed. The captain announced the time of arrival, which was in 10 minutes. Everyone had to be seated with seat belts on for the landing. This was reality. We would soon be on the Island of my birth. I felt overwhelmed to achieve this great opportunity to return to where I came from. I could feel the excitement of a bubbling, warm feeling that travelled up to my chest.

I took deep breaths and closed my eyes. The plane reduced its speed, going down slowly. My ears started popping, and Sabrina started gripping my hand. Looking over at Mum, I could see she was holding the arms of the chair and Crystal was holding her hand. Marsha's face was turned in my direction and she said, "Mummy." I told her it was ok and we would soon land and hold on to Crystal's hand too. We then landed and the speed of the plane slowed down gradually to a standstill.

We had to find a hotel for the night. Then Mum said we have cousins in Antigua. We got a bus to Samuel's family home. We were greeted and found out that Samuel wasn't at home because he had gone to visit family in America. His family greeted us and made us feel at home. After speaking for some time, we all realised that we were at the wrong family's house! It was too late to go to a hotel. This family was very kind and told us we could stay. It was hilarious but could have been a disaster.

Marsha wanted to see what the town was like. Crystal said she would stay with Mum and Sabrina. We went out into the town only to a wine bar that was having karaoke night. Marsha sang a few songs and they all loved her singing. We had a few drinks and returned to the house by taxi. Mum, Crystal, and Sabrina were fast asleep and we then went to bed. In the morning, we showered and they kindly fed us breakfast.

I told them we were so thankful and I was willing to give them some money for putting us up for the night. They refused but I told one of the women to take my watch, which I had just bought. She could keep it as a reminder of them being so kind to us. She accepted it and I was happy. We got a bus and returned to the airport. We boarded the aeroplane to continue our journey from Antigua to St. Kitts, then Nevis. We arrived at St. Kitts and then had to wait for a plane to Nevis.

We were very surprised to see such a small plane that seated about 15 people. It looked tiny compared to the aircraft from England. I didn't want to make anyone scared so I kept my thoughts to myself. I knew everyone else was thinking the same, but didn't want to acknowledge how small this plane was or my thoughts of, *Will we be safe in it?*

I started praying the minute I saw it. As we were setting off, it felt very light and I could see the sharks and big fish. It was very worrying. Looking down brought back memories of my journey to England when I was six. It took fifteen minutes of taking deep breaths, feeling so anxious and trying to be the strong one. Everyone else was scared but tried to be brave. When we landed, it was bumpy and when it stopped, I wanted to shout, "Thank you, God, for getting us here safe!" but I said it to myself. I was concerned for Mum and asked her, "Are you ok Mum?"

"Yes, Ronnie, I travelled on one of these when I came home the last time." She seemed very calm, which I was happy about.

When we got off, Crystal said, "Oh, mummy I was so scared.

"That little plane is not nice. Did you see those sharks?" said Marsha.

"I was very concerned seeing those sharks. I was praying we would be ok." I spoke. Sabrina was holding on to me tight throughout my poor baby; this was an experience and a half.

Coming off that plane was great. The sun was beating down on us. I felt like kissing the ground but resisted. We were on the Island of my birth. It made me feel I belonged. I felt so happy within and a joy at being on this island of paradise. We went through customs. The queue was not lengthy.

We then made our way out of the airport. We got on a bus and observed the scenery. There were palm trees, coconut trees, mango trees, apple trees and so many other fruits I didn't know the names of. Some houses were big and some were small. There were people walking, some were sitting on walls just watching people, some people sitting on their porches, watching buses and cars passing. The roads were very clean. It was a different lifestyle here.

Everyone looked very chilled and contented. The driver spoke as we drove down a long road stretching into the distance. "Your destination is all the way down this road. We are nearly there."

"Ok," I said and tried to look where we were going.

"We are nearly there," the driver said again. "Where you see that wall with a tap, which is where your family live."

Mum said, "Yes, we are here. God, thank you for getting us here safely."

"Amen!" we all said and got out of the bus. I paid the driver, thanked him and he drove off.

I saw a slim woman wearing a dress. She wore her hair tied back and sported a big smile. She came out to greet us. This must be my Aunty Virginia. I ran up to her and hugged her. "Hello aunty Virginia, nice to see you again." I got the impression she was a quiet soul.

She hurried to get over to mum and said hello, how are you? You looking good, though." It appeared that aunty wasn't one for hugs. "Come in out of the sun," she said and helped pull the cases into the house.

The house looked nothing like I remembered. There was a veranda that led to the front room, which had a three-piece suite and a TV. Behind the sofas was the kitchen with a cooker, a sink, and a window you could look out of as you're washing up. The cupboards were high and low all around the kitchen. The was also a fridge freezer. The room was very compact and looked very nice. Then the door knocked and there was my other Aunty Evie. "Hello, everyone. I'm so glad to see you all." I went over and hugged her. Aunty Evie seemed to be friendly. She came across as very cheerful and warm. I was drawn to her from that first day I met her. Mum was exhausted and I asked Aunty Virginia if Mum could have something to eat first. I could sense my mum was overwhelmed with joy at seeing her sisters and being on the Island of her birth. The memories that had run through her mind and opened up so much for her. Looking at Mum, I saw she was so happy, but tired. In the Caribbean, the time was 3pm, compared to 10am in the UK, due to our travel since 8am the previous day. It was a long day for Mama.

After eating, I assisted Mum to the bedroom, making sure she was showered and comfortable in bed. We stayed a while with Mum and she fell asleep. I checked on her frequently. We returned to the room where everyone was. Aunty Virginia spoke about when I was a child. "Apparently, your mum was a very good girl. Her and Emma, they didn't cause no trouble", said my Aunty Virginia. It was good to hear about my childhood and to hear Emma mentioned. I prepared dinner quickly, so we all had dinner. The time flew by and we were exhausted. Aunty Virginia showed us our rooms. We showered and went to bed.

The next day was bright and sunny. We all were up and excited to go out to see the Island. I made breakfast, got mum ready and gave her some breakfast with aunty. We all had breakfast and showered. Then Aunty Virginia told us, "If you go out in half an hour, the bus will be here to pick up people over there," as she pointed to the wall with the water pipe.

"Tell the driver to drop you in town. From there, you can see the pier. That is where you get the bus back. You can walk around the town, which isn't big and people will know you're from England. No one will trouble you."

As we walked around the town area. People were watching us, knowing we were from aboard. Some asked us where we were from. "England." I said.

Then the next question would be, "Who is your family?" When I told them, they would smile and then say, "Oh, ok, enjoy your time while you're here."

"Thanks, we will." Everyone was friendly.

They also would say, "Good morning, or good afternoon." We loved it. The sun was boiling and we had to go under a tree to cool off. We saw a lot of people doing it so we did too. We brought some fruit, a bit of food shopping and things that we needed, then got the bus home. Aunty Virginia and Mum were on the veranda when we got off the bus. Mum looked like she was in her element. She was smiling and looked so happy speaking to her sister. It was great to see them together.

In the evening, we went out with our cousins, who arranged the transport. They lived on the same land as my aunty. After dinner we got ready, as we planned to go out at 8pm. Before going out, I made sure Mum and Sabrina were ready for bed and ok before we left. We were excited and ready to see how the nightlife was in the West Indies.

We were taken to a wine bar and it was karaoke night. A lot of singing and dancing. The stars shimmered in the night sky. It was very warm, with a wonderful cool breeze. This was paradise. It made me think of how distraught I felt to leave this wonderful island at the age of six. This is phenomenal. We danced and Marsha sang a few songs and was applauded. We had a great time. A few guys came over and asked us, "Do you come from England? How long are you here for?" As we were going somewhere else, these three guys followed us.

One of them came up to me. He thought we were all sisters and couldn't get his head round the fact that I was the mother of Crystal and Marsha. It made me feel good, but I was always told that I looked young for my age. This handsome man came up to me. He was very muscular. I couldn't believe he was coming to speak to me. Then, when I realised Crystal and Marsha also had guys speaking to them too, I grabbed hold of their hands and we walked until we got to another bar. We had a fantastic time, filled with laughter and dancing, and as the night ended, we each received phone numbers from young men. When we got in, we were talking about our first night's experience. How excited we were to be here and to make blessed memories together!

In the morning, we got up with the sun and warmth. I helped prepared breakfast for everyone. Everything seemed different to me. I found myself thinking about when I was young. The door that my grandmother held on to would have been in the dining room area. I could see her in my mind and felt sorrow and churning in my stomach. As I went to the back door, the trees with guineps, mangoes, and coconuts were almost ripe. The land went on and on, up high on a hill. At this time, the sun was beating down beautifully. One of our cousins was taking us out later, but we were going to town again first to look around. Getting the bus was different, because there were no bus stops and people would just hold out their hand if they wanted the bus. Getting off the bus in town didn't feel strange today. We recognised certain places; we had passed yesterday. This time, we took Sabrina with us; she was very excited.

She was six, and everything fascinated her. She asked, "What's that, Mummy?" If I knew, I would tell her, and if not, I told her we would have to ask the shop assistant. "My name is Rose; can I help you all?"

"Yes, please can you tell us what these different breads are they here?" "I can give you a taste if you wish?" I agreed and then tasted the different ones. There was a sweet one, fruit ones, and plain ones, which were also very nice. We settled for the sweet bread and a plain one. All of them were delicious and Crystal, Marsha, Sabrina and me, couldn't get over the distinct taste of the cakes. We had a great time tasting the fresh bread and cakes, too. I purchased and took home.

We picked up cheese and eggs and salami to make sandwiches for lunch. I packed tins of tuna, sardines, corn beef in our cases so we could use them for sandwiches. The smell of the wonderful aroma of fresh baked bread was so nice. It reminded me of when Mama used to bake; it brought back memories of my childhood. I had to buy some; it was absolutely out of this world. At this time, I wasn't worried about calories or putting on weight. Anything I wanted, I had. People looked at us as we passed. They would sit down, talking. Most of them would say good afternoon, which felt so nice. We got the bus back to the house.

We then returned home to see Mum and Aunty Virginia sitting and talking on the veranda. My Mum was older than my aunty Virginia and my aunty Evie was the eldest. I told Mum and Aunty that we bought bread, cakes, and mango, apple, and low calorie drinks for Mama and Aunty if they wanted. Mum said, "Yes please, Ron." My Aunty also wanted some. Crystal and Marsha did the sandwiches.

We rested, and then after I helped to prepare the dinner.

17.
GOLD CHAIN AND ANCHOR

Our cousin had a car, and we went to a bar for a drink. There weren't many people in the bar, but I saw the guy who gave me his number. He looked very smart. His shirt and trousers were black, with a small black belt. He wore a gold chain with an anchor on it. He had a broad smile and great teeth. His hair was short and well groomed, with a small parting slightly off the centre. He was slick, with brown skin, dark brown eyes, long eyelashes, thickish eyebrows, a straight nose, and full lips with a small tache and a short goatee beard. He said, "Hello, I'm so glad to see you again," and gave me a kiss on my cheek. He was a bit taller than I. "How are you enjoying the West Indies?"

"It's paradise. I love it! How are you and what's your name again?"

"Oh yes, my name is Douglas... and what's your name?"

"My name is Vee."

"When I saw you, I thought you come across as a very nice person. I have to get to know you."

"Ok, do you say that to all the girls?"

"No, I only tell the truth."

"Good, I love people who tell me the truth."

"Yes, there's no point saying something if it's not true. What do you want to do tonight? There is a few things going on, or do you want to ask your daughters so we can all choose? Can I say though, I was shocked when I heard they were your daughters. You look great honestly. That is the truth."

"Oh, thanks." He was very polite and respectful to me.

We all decided to go to the karaoke bar. They were playing some great music. I really enjoyed Douglas's company. He was very attentive to me all night. I would catch him looking at me, which caused me to feel shy, like a little girl. He knew that because I giggled. I liked Douglas and found him pleasant. The girls were with the guys who gave them their numbers.

The girls and I went out occasionally and it was nice to see them enjoying themselves. We all were speaking to the guys we had just met. It felt strange to me. The girls were watching me all the time and between us, our body language was sending silent messages to each other. Our facial expressions and eye contact and smiles sent cosmic messages. It was so good to watch; the dynamics were so powerful.

Douglas spoke to me regarding his intentions and goals. We started dancing and speaking, which was really nice. Suddenly, it was time to go home. On the way home, there were donkeys running alongside the car. The driver said that they were wild, but they would do nothing to hurt us. It was very unsettling. I didn't know what was going on. After a while, they stopped chasing the car. We got home in one piece. We all arranged for the next day, and said our goodbyes to our new friends, and the three of us entered the house. When we got in, everyone was sleeping and we got ready for bed.

I didn't feel I had slept. The smell of breakfast woke me up. I had a conversation with Mum and Sabrina, and Aunty.

Aunty Virginia made sure they were all ok. After getting something to eat, I went back to bed for a rest. The girls and I spoke about last night and how we felt it went. We all decided that the evening was a great success and the guys were brilliant company.

One day I rang my cousin to let him know when we could visit my other family on the other island, St Kitts, which was 15 minutes away. We went over and stayed for a few nights. Whilst we were getting off the boat, to our surprise Marsha saw Carlos! We were all so glad to see him. He told us he was in the West Indies because his brother had died. I was so sad for him. We exchanged numbers so he could come over to see us for a day. We spoke for a while and our cousin came for us, and we left.

We were on this island of St Kitts for a few days. My cousin Charles had visited the UK and stayed with me. I made sure I looked after him in every way. So, Charles made sure he looked after us by taking us out and showing us around the Island. He took us to two bars and a dance. He took us to the beach. We were taken to different parts of the Island to see a variety of places. We visited family, my dad's sisters, my aunties, meeting them for the first time.

This was an eye opener for me. They were all in their late fifties now. They asked about Dad and told me he used to hit them a lot and would laugh. They were glad to meet me and to see me, but there was no talk of them giving me a number or suggestion to call them or to keep in touch. Charles looked after us and made us feel welcome. We had a great time.

Even though we enjoyed ourselves, I missed Douglas, Crystal, Marsha, and Sabrina missed going to the beach with Douglas and the other guys. The Girls missed their friends on the island of Nevis too. Whilst I was in St Kitts, Carlos rang me and we decided for him to come over with us when we were going back to Nevis. He came over for a few hours to Nevis. We showed him around the town and we all sat with him until he was ready to go. I could tell he would have loved to have stayed longer. Insufficient rooms and my aunt's strict rules against unmarried guests presented a problem. Even though we were friends, I still don't think she would have been comfortable with it. He understood that anyway. I could see he wanted to be with us longer. Carlos and I were only friends at this time. We hugged and gave each other a kiss on the cheek and said our goodbyes. I watched the boat leave until I couldn't see him, as we all waved him off.

The next day, we were taken to the beach in Nevis for most of the day. Sabrina came with us. She enjoyed the experience and Douglas was very good with her. He had a great sense of humour with the girls, too. There were two cars to take us around Nevis, as Carlos promised. The two guys, Liam and James, were in one car. Sabrina was with me and Douglas and the girls were with James and Liam. We all went to the seaside first. We swam and sunbathed and spent an hour, then dried off and changed before we were driven around the Island by following each other in the cars. We would stop for something to eat and a drink and have a conversation and stretch our legs before continuing the journey together. The blazing sun and the car's air conditioning created ideal conditions. I had brought us the sandwiches and drinks as the guy got the cars. I felt it was only fair to contribute even though Douglas said he didn't want me to do that; I told him I really wanted to contribute. The Island was beautiful and the scenery was phenomenal. Looking at the deep blue sea reminded me of going onto the ship at the age of 6yrs. Now looking at it from where I am at this age, it's not that frightening; it's beautiful and calm. It gave me a sense of peace.

Douglas was a nice person; we got on very well. We spoke about situations that bothered us about former relationships and what we needed in a partner. Four weeks were slipping by. Because of the time we had, it felt that being honest and speaking about things that really mattered was very important. He told me about someone he originally met and who was very kind to him and his family. I told him that if he felt she was the one for him, he shouldn't hold back because life was too short for games. I knew there was some chemistry between us; it felt very strong. I asked him, "Do you feel the same?"

He replied, "Yes." He was now thinking about what to do.

It felt like I was living in one of the movies I've always watched. Two singles find love, but is it real or just a fun holiday fantasy? All I knew was this was a wonderful feeling that I had never experienced in my life and it was happening to me. This handsome, thoughtful, caring man, with a brilliant smile and a body every woman would dream of, was here with me, loving me back. He was kind and loving and it seemed like a fairytale. He drove the car up a hill and the view was breathtaking. The sea and the moonlight met. What a moment; it felt complete. Nothing else mattered at this present time. Our favourite song came on the radio, *Breathe Again* by Toni Braxton: -

...

He held me in his arms and told me, "This is our song. This is our moment. No one can take this from us. We can remember this in our hearts forever. The moment we hear the words of this song. Wherever we are in this world, our hearts can meet together." This moment felt so real, like nothing could ever stop us from remembering what we felt. The tingling feeling in my stomach travelled throughout my whole being. It was so strong it almost took my breath away. This wonderful moment of feeling loved. I felt it was great to have this experience than to go through life never knowing such feelings existed.

One day, while we went for a drive, we visited his brother's house. We stayed for a while. As we talked about his needs, the conversation revealed a striking resemblance in our life goals and the things we hoped to achieve. We looked at each other and in that moment I felt all these feelings of joy, feeling my heart pounding in my chest. These are the moments I cherish, experiencing such kindness and gentleness from this handsome, thoughtful man in paradise.

After a year Douglas came over to the UK. One day he just walked into the salon, I couldn't believe it. He came and picked me up and hugged me. We had time together, but just as friends, as he was seeing someone. He knew I was going to respect that person a hundred per cent.

We spoke about his experiences in the UK and when he saw me out, he would come up to me and say hello. I ran into Douglas again in the West Indies sixteen years later. He was married to a local woman. He told me he had changed his life and he was now a Christian; I was happy for him. This was the last time I saw Douglas. I went back since then but didn't see him. I will always thank him for the memories we have for life.

When I came back from the West Indies. I realised Carlos was on the same flight. I was very upset and down because I was missing Douglas. I think Carlos sensed my sadness and figured I was upset about someone. What made me even more upset was that our flight was delayed for another day. I just wanted to go back and spend the last moments with Douglas.

18.
From Paradise to Reality

Coming back to reality, the salon was in trouble. My clients came back and told me they were glad I was back and shared their views with me. I had to work very hard because things weren't good financially. As time passed, my dad had to be taken into care for his health and wellbeing. I visited him often. Mum was ok and still had Sabrina at weekends. On Saturday after work, I'd pop over to check they had their church clothes ready and enough money for the taxi. I would then go home and get ready and join friends at parties or clubs. Most of the time, I stayed local. I would go to parties on my own because there was always someone I knew there. Plus, I would drive, so I wouldn't drink and that was ok with me.

One night, I ran into Martin from church and said hello. On this particular night, we started speaking about church and people we knew. The conversation went on and he invited me to his place. Usually, I wouldn't go to anyone's house at that time of night. I felt I could trust him; we had a drink, and he told me he had lost his mum and he wasn't in a good place. He expressed loss and loneliness and I was also lonely. We both craved a listening ear and a friend; we needed to feel heard. We were talking and ended up laying down on the bed fully clothed and fell asleep. I woke up. I didn't wake him but left. This was fine with me, because I only needed a friend at this time. We saw each other often but never mentioned that night.

Until 25yrs later, I mentioned it. We had a laugh, he said, he regretted that nothing happened. Looking back, we both gained from that time; it was a safe and caring environment where someone was there to listen.

I continued working hard to build up the business again. A client came into the salon and told me about counselling. She said there was a need for Black counsellors. I felt that this would be good and I would look into it. I put this on the back burner as I was very concerned about the salon. I decided to offer skincare classes to draw more clients to the salon, hoping the educational aspect would attract a new clientele. I started with offers. People started coming and the skin care was successful. It was all about getting people to know I was here and offer a service that was different. I got trainees in to gain experience. Some were serious and some weren't.

Meanwhile, I hired Sophie, Crystal's friend, to help Crystal braid clients' hair at the salon while I drove to London for a hair show. I took C5ystal, Marsha, Sophie and Leo, Marsha's boyfriend at the time. This was about learning about new business products and their uses. When the hair show had finished, there was a party going on; we passed through and stopped at the party for a few hours. It went on until morning. We had to sleep in the car for a few hours before driving back home. I came back with new products and new ideas. Eventually, the salon picked up and became busy again. The practice of praying and trusting in God never left me. Crystal was very busy with the plaiting. There were many people coming in for plaits. I became busy again and acquired new clients all the time. Sometimes we would finish very late, so I got more staff to help with the plaiting and other hairdressing techniques.

I went out to a party one night and met Ralph, who came from London. He was dark-skinned, and handsome, with a broad smile, good teeth, and a nice presence. He asked me for a dance. As we were dancing, he asked, "Who did you come with?"

"I came with my two daughters."

"Ok, where are they?"

"These are my daughters." I pointed them out since they were close by.

"They are your daughters?" He put his hand to his mouth in shock. "I can't believe you have grown-up daughters! I don't normally ask a lady her age but, How old are you?"

"I'm 38."

He was so surprised, with his mouth open, he looked me up and down. "Wow, you don't look it at all!" I told him that most people thought I was much younger than my age. I sensed he liked me and he wasn't bad looking either. We had a few dances, and he could really dance. He had a sense of humour and was very polite. We also asked each other where we were from originally and where we lived now. I then knew he was born in Africa and lived in London and that he was with his friend. I noticed he had a slight stutter. We danced for the rest of the night and exchanged numbers. We then left and I said goodbye.

Ralph called me the next day to see if I was free for a drink or to go out the following weekend. "Okay, that would be nice," I said.

"Where do you want to go? My friend will take me there and pick me up. That's not a problem." "Ok, can I get back to you tomorrow?"

"Ok, I just want to say it was a pleasure meeting you last night. Have a good day, and I look forward to hearing from you tomorrow?"

"Okay, talk soon," I said before ending the call.

We ended up going out with each other for two years. We would visit each other. We took it in turn going to each other's houses every two weeks. I would finish work at the salon. Make sure Sabrina and Mum were ok, before going over to London. I would pack and drive after work on the Saturday and return on Sunday night to take Sabrina to school on Monday morning. This went on for one and a half years. Ralph asked me to marry him. We had a discussion regarding where we would live and how this marriage would work.

Someone had to move and it couldn't be me, because of my mother, daughter and business. We discussed it and Ralph gave up his job and life in London to marry and live with me. He started looking for work in Leeds from London. He wanted to have a job before he began living with me in Leeds. He also wanted residence here. This was very different for me. I knew what could happen; him getting his residency and leaving me. I had to know this relationship was not a marriage of convenience. I told him how I felt and he had to speak to my mum, my daughters, as they were my life. I wasn't prepared to keep anything hidden. He then spoke with all the important individuals.

We decided together to go ahead with this marriage because we loved each other and respected each other enough, to be honest. Within another year, we were married at the register office. Something seemed strange that day. After the marriage, he didn't let me see the marriage certificate. I couldn't understand why. Until months later, I mentioned it and told him I need to see it. He told me he had sent it off for his stay. I didn't let it go and knew I had to ask his father straight up, as he was in the UK, "How old is Ralph?" he told me he was younger than me but I felt he was even younger than he said he was. His father told me it was not up to him to turn over his apple cart. I understood and was very upset.

I left the house that day and was heading home to Leeds. Ralph was still living in London at the time. I went to a pub to gather my thoughts. "What am I going to do?" Looking up, I saw Ralph come into the pub. He convinced me not to go home upset.

I said to him, "You're younger than you told me you were. How young are you?"

"Let's go home and I'll tell you everything."

"No, I'm staying here until you tell me your age. How old are you?" Then he told me he was four years younger than he had told me previously. "Right, you will have to tell my mum that too! I don't know why you felt you had to lie. All you needed to do was to be honest and give me that choice, to say yes or no." I decided to go home the next day.

We agreed he would come up to Yorkshire on Friday and speak to my mum about this situation.

He came and we both went to see my mum. My mum has always been fair and told the truth as she saw it. She told me, "I know Ralph didn't tell you the truth. As he said, he felt if he told you his proper age, you wouldn't have married him."

She then turned to Ralph. "Do you love Veronica? Or did you marry her for convenience? Tell her the truth. No more lies, because lies always come out and it destroys lives." He then told Mum that he loved me and that he would never lie to me again.

"I hope you don't, because once you do anything like this again. I will not be in this marriage and I mean it." I then let this go but meant every word. We were ok for a few years. We made sure we had a break together each year to celebrate our anniversary.

I knew Crystal was expecting her first baby and told her to inform me if she went into labour, so I could head back home. I knew her partner was with her and would ensure she was fine. One day, I received a call that Crystal was in labour. After hours of waiting, she had a baby girl, my first grandchild. I felt truly blessed and couldn't wait to meet my granddaughter. Crystal and her partner had been together for some time. Getting home, I was so excited and happy. Since the news, I couldn't stop smiling, butterflies in my stomach, full of joy. We went to see my wonderful granddaughter. She was just perfect. I kissed and hugged this wonderful baby and my daughter. My granddaughter had very dark skin, with a lot of hair, and big, beautiful eyes looking back at me. I felt like I was the richest grandmother alive. What a blessing and so much joy.

I noticed Ralph was changing a bit. He went out without me. He would go out with his friend and his friend's girlfriend. They were like the three musketeers. He would leave the house around 11am and come back to collect his clothes for work at 7.00pm. He was training to be a nurse. I told him that I was not happy with his using the house as a hotel. He didn't meet me halfway. I felt now he had his residency; he felt free to do and act as he pleased. He didn't respect me or the home.

Sabrina was here and he would promise her he would take her to town many times and disappointed her every time. This alone upset me when I saw the disappointment and despair in the eyes of my 11-year-old child. I know that this didn't help Sabrina and left her wanting a father figure. When me and Sabrina's father finished. It felt like he finished with his girls, too. He went to London and didn't bother with any of them. Sabrina was three or four when we divorced.

Ralph was doing the same thing. He used to promise her to take her out each week and never did. This contributed to a lot of problems later in life. He was out all the time. One day I called him and he told me he was at a pub. I didn't have a car at the time. My friend visited and I asked her to take me to this pub. My daughter didn't know what was going on. Since her friend was over, I let her know I was going out but wouldn't be gone long. I went to the pub. There was no sign of him. This proved my feelings were right. I then called him, "Are you still at the pub?"

He answered, "Yes, I am."

"I'm coming up there in a taxi." I said. He told me not to because he is coming now.

On my return, my friend dropped me off at the end of my street. I came back into the house and my daughter and friend were ok.

I told her I would be back in 20 minutes.

On my way to my friends within five minutes from my house. I saw Ralph's car. I continued walking. He drove up and stopped the car instantly, which caused a squeaking noise. Ralph started shouting at me. I didn't stop walking and said, "Why are you airing your problems in the street?" and hoped this was enough for him to stop shouting. I continued walking until I reached my friend's house (Suzy). I told her what had happened and she gave me what I needed, a sensitive ear, so I could speak and get to a conclusion about how to move forward. She was like my elder sister. I will always be thankful for her support.

I returned home within 15 minutes, as my daughter and her friend Mia were in the house. I realised they detected nothing. I went upstairs to find Ralph. on the bed, in an upright position and breathing heavily. I said nothing and started moving my clothes out of the wardrobe. He watched without speaking. After taking all the clothes I needed, I closed the door and returned to the other bedroom. I then stayed in the next bedroom for weeks. Ralph realised I was not backing down in this situation. I had been through this before and felt that I needed to be very careful about how I acted because of my daughter's emotional state.

I didn't want her to see anything that would cause further distress. One day, Ralph stooped and kissed my feet. I'd had enough and this meant nothing to me. I felt deeply hurt by his behaviour. He had disrespected me and I decided not to take anymore abuse from him or anyone. I had to look after my daughter's mental health. One night he told me, "I don't have to move out. I can live here as long as I want."

"Not without paying and contributing to the bills." I stated. He started smiling. I didn't want to get too upset and say anything that I wasn't sure about. To avoid giving him ammunition, I got some advice. I told him as long as you continue to contribute to the bills, that's ok. It went on for a while and the week he didn't put the money to contribute towards the bills was the time I packed all his 15 bags of clothes.

I had my grandchildren with me that night. I left the key in the lock and he couldn't open the door until he rang the bell in the morning. Ralph came in and brushed past me. I told him, "Don't push past me." Crystal had two children. The eldest granddaughter was three years and the second grandson Crystal had was two years.

The children spent the night with me. Crystal was getting the children ready for nursery and came out of the room. He was shocked when he saw her and said nothing. All the bags were placed at the entrance. I had clients that day, since I was now working from home. Crystal moved the bags to the back room and briefly left before returning while I worked next door, where my salon was located. Inside, a fitted cupboard on the left stored products and rollers. There was one dryer and one steamer for treatments. A shampoo unit, there were cupboards fitted high on the wall straight ahead with all the clean towels. Lower down on the wall, there were two mirrors on either side of the wall, with the chairs in front. There was magazines tray between each unit on the floor, for clients to look at the latest hairstyles. There was a cabinet locked for storing personal details in the corner, with a large plant on top, which was my mum's plant (from 26 years ago). There was the window and a small table that also had more magazines next to a settee for clients to sit until their service. On the wall above were certificates, and below the certificates was a TV so clients can watch TV or listen to music. It was very private and comfortable for my clients.

Sabrina was off school, and Ralph had the cheek to send her to the shop for black bags. I went into the back room. There were so many clothes piled on the floor. I looked at him and he looked at me. I returned to work. Next, I saw Ralph packing things in his car, which was completely full. He left. The next thing was to get a locksmith to change all the locks.

I was sad about this relationship ending. Weeks later Ralph tried to be apologetic. I felt he regretted the way we finished. I invited him to the house after I had redecorated the dining room. This was my way of acknowledging, in a quiet yet powerful way, that I had persevered, a silent testament to my survival. As long as I have my faith, this is who I am. After this, we didn't see each other for a while and met up when we felt like it, but he never moved back in.

I began to eat more healthily and stopped eating fatty foods. I lost weight and went down two dress sizes. I felt I had let myself go by eating his fatty foods with a lot of oil. I needed a dress and had to go to Evans plus size boutique. I stood there thinking; *I don't want this for me.* I had to get something because all of my clothes didn't fit me anymore. Sabrina was with me and I felt my feet wouldn't move towards the railings. I then made a verbal promise and said to Sabrina, "I will not come back in here for nothing else."

I bought a skirt and wore it and had it for years to remind myself how I felt that day. I felt broken and sad that I had done this to myself. I wanted to look beautiful and slim for myself, no one else but myself. I told myself I will not do this because my health depends on it. I want to live to see all of my grandchildren and run around with them. I was an 18 plus and I'm now a size 12/14, which I love and will not do that to myself again. I go to the gym; I walk and make sure I exercise every day. Even ten squats daily help me to maintain my mental health and agility.

I had to give myself space to heal and allow God to bring someone into my life who would be right for me and me for that person. Where there would be happiness, peace, joy and, above all, spiritual satisfaction. So, my daughters would observe what true love looks like.

I got my decree absolute on my birthday. I felt sad for both of us but knew that it was for the best.

Years later I saw Ralph in a Clarks shoe shop with Sabrina and her children. Seeing Sabrina with her own children surprised him. He offered to contribute some money towards the grandchildren's shoes. I felt this was a token of consolation. Years after this, I met him at the gym. We spoke. It's wonderful to acknowledge the people who have been in my life. At times, things were very good and sometimes bad. This is part of life. The good and the bad caused me to learn and grow. This is life. After nine years together, we got divorced.

19.
MAMA GOING INTO THE HOME

Shortly after this, my mother became unable to care for herself. It broke my heart. I closed the salon and set up at home, where I could manage my responsibilities better. I had Sabrina. I had my business. Mum was my priority, as she needed me more than ever. I wanted to bring her home with me but things were not good with Ralph.... and I knew I just couldn't manage it all. The decision to place my mother in a home was heartbreaking.

I wasn't supported by anyone and felt that I was completely alone except for my girls and a few friends who helped me to stay focused and kept me in prayer. I had to give up the shop so I could have more time to look after my mum. I Still had Sabrina, who was very venerable and appeared to be very quiet and spoke little about anything. Crystal and Marsha still needed me. I visited my mum more often to make sure she was being looked after by the carers in the home. I would pop up to the care home at any time. My father was also in the same care home, but he didn't recognise my mother and my mum didn't really know he was there because of dementia. Seeing it caused me profound sorrow, but it was my reality. I visited my father but every time he would start arguing with me.

All the girls and I went to see Mama regularly. We would spend an hour with her. She was happy in this home; she was clean and looked contented. The staff were very good with her, as she didn't give anyone any trouble. I would go at different times, so they would expect me anytime of the day or early evening. Sometimes I would turn up just before Mum was going to bed. Ralph used to go with me. Mum always enjoyed seeing Ralph. He also liked going seeing her. Sabrina would go with me most of the time.

Having my father in the same home seemed convenient, as I could see both parents. However, he often argued and misbehaved, especially toward me.

Dementia eventually left my parents unaware of each other's presence in the same facility, my father in one room and my mother in another. I was informed that my father was in hospital and that my uncle planned to take him out for a drink. I advised my father not to go with his brother for drinks.

"Yes, ok", he replied. I could feel that Dad knew it was wrong but got influenced by his brother. His brother was a very angry and very violent person and felt he was always right. I had nothing to do with him.

One day I was in the house and heard someone come in. I was shocked to see my uncle standing there at the entrance. He began to be very abusive; he had a terrible temper. "What are you doing in my house and coming up to me? Get out of my house. How dare you just walk in? Get out or I will call the police now, get out now!" I felt he was going to hit me. As Ralph came out of the kitchen, he ran out of the door. As I went to lock the door, I discovered there was a smell of dog faeces. It was on the carpet. He brought this into the house. I couldn't believe anyone could do such a thing. Ralph couldn't believe it. We cleaned it up. I was so upset. He shouted, "You're not getting any of my brothers' money." What he didn't realise was that I didn't want any money. I just wanted a peaceful life without stress. If I need money, as long as I'm in good health, I can get my own.

My father became worse and when I went to see him, I was told by the doctor that he was dying. I was very upset and the doctor asked me if I wanted to tell him. "Yes, I will, Doctor, so there's nothing you can do for him?"

"Nothing, I'm sorry."

"Ok, thank you." I went to see him. "It was the hardest thing I had to tell him. I was broken with grief, knowing I was going to lose my one and only father on this earth. I really loved my dad even though he'd treated my mum and me badly so many times. He was still my dad and I still loved him. My heart was broken to hear this news and now I had to tell him. The pain I felt was so bad and I never heard my dad tell me he loved me once. I knew he did really but it was such a shame that he didn't say, "I love you, my daughter," not once, never.

When I eventually built up the courage to tell my father he was dying, he said, "Am I Ma? Did the doctor tell you this?"

"Yes, Daddy," I knew he was broken.

Then he said, "I'm so sorry for how I treated you and your mum."

"It's ok Daddy, it's ok Daddy."

"Please tell your mother for me."

"Yes, I will, Daddy."

"It's that Lance that cause me to do it."

"Don't worry, Daddy, as long as you give your life to Jesus. That's all we want you to do, Daddy."

"Yes, ma, yes." I had never seen my dad so obedient and humble.

"I love you, Daddy and all I want is for you to give your life to Jesus. That's all, Daddy."

"Yes, Ma Yes." I prayed with my dad, and he made that commitment to God and I knew he meant it. I visited soon after. I read the Bible and sang to him. I couldn't… I just didn't want to see him die. I went home late that night; this was the last time I felt my father squeeze my hand.

As I write this, I'm crying for my father and me. He may not have had his father; tell him he loved him either. How sad to go through life with the most important people in your life and not hear those precious words. I love you. It shows how important it is to tell the people you love that you love them and treasure the moments, the times we are together in love. Without this, so many lives are destroyed.

I felt so sad that our relationship was not a loving one. I knew he loved me but he didn't show me at all or tell me. This was such a shame, now I have grown, I understand you can't teach what you haven't learned. Now I'm at peace with it, because God has allowed me to see through my father's hardship of having to deal with his mother's death at the age of 13.

He was left with four siblings to bring up and he was just a child. He never mentioned a father in his life. It would have been hard to keep all of his siblings together, plus feeding and clothing them. Dad, I love you because I understand it now, and this may be the foundation, which was pain, anger, not trusting, and being hard. You built a wall so high that no one can climb or look over it. The wall you had was to stop others from coming in, or to look over, because it was so tall. It's so hard to live in isolation, because you didn't let anyone in.

20.
My Father's Funeral

My father died. My uncle organised the funeral. He didn't have the decency to consider my mother, who was still my father's wife. There wasn't any space in the car for her. It gave him joy when he saw us struggling to get Mum up the stairs of the church. Later, I heard he told the minister not to allow me to say anything at the funeral. I was not upset. I just sang my heart out for my dad and felt sorry for my uncle and his ignorance. A friend took my mum to the cemetery. I was late because I had to find someone to give me a lift. One of my family members wanted to embarrass me by telling me off for leaving my mother standing and waiting for so long. I told her, "Go back to where you were. She is also your mother. Why didn't you get the wheelchair out of the car?" She just walked away full of shame. At this point, I'd just had enough of everything.

That night I thought about the whole funeral and could still see my uncle's face gloating as we tried to get Mum up the stairs of the church. The hate on his face with a smug stare. I then thought about my father and what he was seeing in the spirit. I prayed God would help my uncle to understand that all this was just unnecessary. We live and then we die. Then we have to give an account of what we have done in our bodies, whilst we were on earth.

Lance had taken my dad to the solicitor and willed all his money to his sisters and possibly to him, too. I was not bothered about any money. I thought if my dad didn't want to give my mum and I, why should I make a fuss now he's died? I just left everything in God's hands. Then I get a call from the solicitors asking me if I knew my auntie's addresses. "No, I replied, I don't want anything to do with any of this."

After a few days I couldn't visit my mum because I was so busy with work. I called every day to make sure Mum was ok. I was very upset to discover no one had told me about this abrasion.

When I visited my mum, she had an ulcer on her right ankle. I asked if the doctor had been called to look at it. I was told, "Yes."

"Who has been dressing this sore?"

One carer in the home said, "We have."

"This is shocking. My Mum has diabetes."

"The nurse should be coming in and dressing the wound." I was so upset with the home. I thought, *the minute I go away for two weeks, this happens.*

I wanted the doctor to see the sore, as my mother had diabetes and was in danger of getting an infection that could lead to amputation.

I rang the doctor and asked if he could come to the home to see my mother's foot. They said the nurse could come. The doctor wasn't very pleased when I asked for a doctor and not a nurse. I didn't care. My mum needed to be taken care of properly. The doctor visited my mother the next day and prescribed some medication. The nurse visited the same day and dressed the wound. The ulcer became bigger and bigger and wouldn't heal. My mum eventually ended up in hospital.

At this time, Crystal was about to have her second child, which Mum knew. I took Crystal to see Mum the day after she was discharged from the Maternity ward. My mum was not well, and I wasn't sure how much time she had left. Mum sat upright and looked over at Crystal. and the baby and laid back down. She was hanging on for Crystal to have the boy that she always wanted.

After this, my Mum was fighting her sickness. A doctor recognised me from the salon, but I didn't remember her until she told me. "You have to release your Mum because she is holding on for you." It was the worst moment of my life. The thought of my Mum leaving me in this world, on my own. Mum, how can I let you go? The doctor told me there was nothing they could do for her.

I had to go back and tell my Mum everything would be ok; "I will be ok Mum. I love you so much but I will be ok...

You have been my rock. Mama, I love you so much. Thank you for being there for me through thick and thin. I will always think of you. You will always be in my heart." I allowed her to go in peace, knowing she heard me say it.

The last thing I never wanted to feel was her being cold. I felt I could never cope with the memory again. I just couldn't. I'm so sorry, my dear mother and dear dad. If I knew that the body cools down gradually. I would have held your hands and prayed with you until the very end. One day we will be together again and everything will be wonderful in the Heavenly Kingdom.

I now had to arrange Mama's funeral; this was the hardest thing I ever had to do. The funeral director was booked. The Church was informed of a date; the reception was also booked; A coach was booked. I was cooking and got some help to serve the food. The drinks would be served by friends who volunteered to help me on the day.

My dear mother was brought to my house that day. I decorated the room with white lace. I couldn't touch my mum because I felt I would remember that memory of coldness forever. I wanted to remember my wonderful Mum, who was warm, loving, kind, and loved me unconditionally.

Ralph invited his family from London. Marsha was singing for her grandma. Crystal had just had her son and didn't feel well on the day. I didn't have any help from my external family.

A few days after Mama's passing, one of my sisters, Julia, demanded we had six cars for the funeral. "No," I replied, as each family had a car. She wasn't pleased. There was one car for my family and another one for my four sisters. Crystal, Marsha, Sebrina, Ralph, and I were in the first car. As we were entering the car, I glanced at my eldest sister and her eldest daughter entering the second car. They greeted me saying, "hello."

I thought as we were driven to the church, thinking, my Mum lived in this area for over 50 years. Now she doesn't need it all anymore. My whole body felt numb. I couldn't believe this was really happening. My precious, wonderful Mama was taking this drive for the last time. I'm now on my own. How will I cope now? A man with a black hat and suit opened the door for me. I saw a crowd of people get out of their cars. It reminded me of a village. There were so many people.

As I got in the front door of the church, I saw my sisters with their children. There may have been 40 of them. All standing together on the left side. They watched us as we entered. Mama's coffin was already near the door. I had a lot of nephews that could have carried their grandma's coffin, but no one came forward.

Ralph said, "Can I carry Mama?"

"Yes," I said, "that would be good." Ralph and the other three pallbearers carried Mama into the church. The service was very intense. Everyone looked at me as I spoke, but my intention was to do the best I could for my dear Mama, who I loved and treasured. I took deep breaths as I continued to say my tribute and expressed my love for my wonderful Mother. Sabrina also wanted to pay tribute to her grandmother, and my friend Violet, who was a true blessing, joined her. Sharing our hardships and joys helped Violet and me through many tough times. I was so grateful to her for supporting Sabrina (Violet was Sabrina's godmother) at this hard time.

At this time all I could think about was why is this happening. Our Mother has died, where is the compassion. Were there any love, sorrow or pain. Our Mother has died and this is her funeral. I couldn't believe how calm everyone looked. My Mother was my life. All I could do is to remain calm and know I had to make my mum proud by reading my notes that I had prepared for my dear Mama. I have to make her proud. I wanted to do my best. I felt others thought I was the favourite but it wasn't the case. I know she loves all her children and grandchildren very much and did the best she could with what she had. I love Mama because, he saved me from my father's belt many a times. She made me understand the importance of taking care of myself. We were very close as I was the last to leave home.

I didn't ever want to upset or disappoint Mama because she helped me to love myself and recognize I can reach the stars. If I work hard enough. I loved Mama with all of my heart. She was kind, friendly, caring and helped so many people who were in need or gave money to many, even though she didn't have much herself. Mama had a big heart for people and didn't tell others who she gave money too. Sometimes I felt some people took advantage of her kindness, even though Mama knew this she gave them anyway. Her moto was Ronnie do the best you can because God sees everything and he will work out everything in his own timing. Just do the right thing. God will repay you with his blessings.

This was the time to put aside every thought of anger, disappointment and dislike. I felt like I was carrying the burden of the whole weight of my world on my shoulders. I felt alone, abundant and hated. I have always tried to be respectful towards my sisters. I felt there were no peace or compassion. How could this be happening. I felt I was in a dream and in a minute this feeling of loneliness and my hurting stomach because I'm now fighting with my thoughts, grief and unbelief. The faces that were watching me would disappear, because it was just a terrible dream.

The time came for the viewing of Mama's body before they closed the coffin. Whoever wanted to come and see Mama, could. I touched one of Mama's friends on the hand to comfort her. To my amazement, she pushed my hand away. I was very shocked by her actions and felt she got drawn into this discomfort too. Before the coffin closed. I went up to see Mama for the last time. My fourth sister Ester voiced her opinion of me. I got the opinion that she felt Mama loved me and saw no wrong in me. That was not the truth. Mama would tell me to do the right thing in life because if you don't, it will come back to you good or bad. I knew I'm not perfect, but I strived to get on with my sisters. I never was rude to any of them.

I was ignored in the street. I continually said hello until I felt enough is enough. I'm also a human being with feelings. I started looking straight ahead and wouldn't say anything. I was done with feeling not good enough and treated unkindly. I also knew that it wasn't right to pass them either. I asked God to give me the courage to handle this situation his way. So, I felt I had to continue to say hello even if I didn't get an answer from any of my sisters. One of my sisters while viewing Mama's body said to Mama "It's all over now. You can rest in peace now," and then giving me the worst look ever. I was so done with every rude comment, every insult. I was so over everything. At the burial, people were singing and the rain was pouring down. Someone told me that rain was a blessing.

We then headed to the reception where drinks and food were available. The minister and most of the people came to the reception. My cousin Stella from Leicester came. There were a lot of people but I didn't see any of the family. After a few hours my two sisters Ester and Melda came through the door and asking people to come with them.

I then realised that there were two receptions going on for Mama at the same time. People were approached to come and join them and refused to go and felt it wasn't necessary. Some people asked me if it's ok if they went. I just told them of course if you wish to go that's fine. I didn't feel anyway, as I knew I did the right thing for my mother without making a fuss. I respected myself and the principles my mother taught me. Don't disrespect my elders and believe in God and be of good courage. God is all powerful and all knowing. He has the answers and the strength we need to face any challenge before us. He was with Joshua, and he will be with us, as in (Joshua 1:9).

Suzy, another friend, was incredibly supportive during my difficult times, and I'm so grateful for her help and encouragement. I had no feeling in my body. I was alive but inside I felt numbness and lifeless. How can I live without my wonderful Mum? How will I cope without her? She was my world. As I thought of my dear mother, there were no words to express the brokenness and emptiness I felt. This all felt unreal and I was waiting to wake up and find it was a terrible dream and none of this had really happened.

As I Started packing up, I questioned myself, *Have I really buried my Mum? Was this hall used for a gathering of her life? What can I do now without her voice and the touch of her soft face? I needed her to tell me how much she loves me, and that I will be ok. Who can I tell my deep feeling, and fears too, how can I ever function again?*

I felt lost in that moment of time. I didn't know what to do with anything. The pain broke me into irreparable pieces, and tears streamed down my face as I recalled Mum's reassurances that I was good enough. As I swept the floor, I sensed a warm feeling in my chest. I looked up to see people still in the hall. It was tidy and how we found it. As we travelled home. It felt like I was floating and I couldn't feel my feet. The reception continued at my house until people were ready to go home. I felt sad and didn't know what to think or say to anyone. I just looked at people, but I was not really present. I was detached from my body, merely observing without engaging. My family came to mind. All I ever wanted and hoped was that we could all get on. It was in the hand of God and I couldn't change anyone's heart. Only God can do that.

Shortly after Ralph and I separated and then got divorced.

I started a course, introduction to counselling and found it fascinating. This course was for 10weeks. I really enjoyed it and enrolled for the next level, which was the Level 2 counselling skills for one year, which I attended one day a week. This course helped me to develop the skills of working with clients through difficulties they may face. I found it very helpful, as I was trying to heal myself again. I felt Ralph had disappointed me by leaving me and going out with his friends too much. I needed a person who would want to be with me for me. To enjoy our lives together, as we know tomorrow, isn't promised to anyone.

I got a lot out of the Level 2 Counselling Skills course. The skills, which reminded me of how we should think and how to treat others intrigued me. This was my way of thinking. After a year of studying this course, I really like the way my tutor taught the subject. His voice was so calm, direct, but used the skills he was teaching on us. I fell in love with the skills and how it impacted my life and the life of others. We had to practise the skills on each other each week. I found it very helpful, as it allowed me to be honest with myself and learn to trust others in the class. We had to be the client, then the counsellor, by using the skills being taught. I passed this course.

I progressed to Level 3, focusing on various psychological methods of counselling. The different techniques that are used to help the client reach their requirements.

I then went on to Level 4. This course was for two years and this level would enable us to be counsellors. I still loved the course and was thankful I had great teachers that really enjoyed and believed in the skills they were teaching. Before finishing this course, I had to go on a 2-day course to put all our learning into practise. This allowed us to use our skills in front of the class, so the tutor could assess our abilities, skills, and our awareness. We had to pass this, to gain our certificate in Level 4 in counselling skills.

While I was away on this course, my friend Ava was with Sabrina for the weekend, making sure she was ok. At this time, Marsha had her own place and was busy working. Crystal was living with her partner and had my granddaughter and grandson to look after. Sabrina was too young to be left on her own. Coming back from the course, I wasn't feeling too well and was glad to be back home.

I was just going to bed when the doorbell rang.. I opened the bedroom window and looked to see who was at the door. To my surprise, it was Carlos. as he looked up and I told him, "I have just come back from a course and I'm so tired, let's catch up another time."

He said, "ok."

"Yes you can come sometime next week."

"ok then. Take care." I then closed the window and waved. Carlos came around during the week. It was good to see him after such a long time. As usual, we picked up where we left off. He was not going out with anyone and neither was I.

21

TAKING IT SLOW...

It was difficult at first because Sabrina didn't really know Carlos like Crystal and Marsha did. She was young and I had to be careful how we would approach this. I told Sabrina about me wanting to have a relationship with Carlos and asked her what she thought? "Well, mum if you like him, it's up to you."

"Yes, I do. I've always liked him, but what do you think?"

"I think he's ok."

Carlos and I started seeing each other but took it slowly. We gave it sometime before we took it to the next level.

I had to think of Sabrina and be responsible for her thinking by showing her how to do things respectfully. I would visit Carlos and he would visit me and leave at night until she saw we were a couple. I never had a man living with me without being married. Eventually it felt ok and Sabrina seemed to be ok with our relationship. To be fair, Carlos was very good with the girls and he became a father figure to Sabrina and she began to really like Carlos. He had this caring, nurturing approach to the girls and, with time. Sabrina began to really like Carlos. He treated her like his own daughter, as he did with Crystal and Marsha.

We would laugh, as Carlos would tell us stories and jokes. He was a joy to have around. We used to play cards, dominos, and more. Sabrina, Carlos and I got on very well together. He'd ask, "Sabrina, Vee, what do you want for breakfast?", then tell us what was downstairs, cook it, and bring it up, especially if I was going to work. Sometimes, I would go downstairs or send Sabrina to help him with whatever he needed help with. It was good to have Carlos. He was a family guy who cared for us all. We had a happy home, with a lot of laughter and fun.

Seeing each other again. I had missed him for his funny jokes and his happy nature. I had missed him so much. We always seem to come back and carry on where we left off. We started seeing each other once a week, then I twice, then more until we were an item again. This was something we couldn't help. We like each other and love came easy for us because the trust was there always.

There were no arguments, no bad feelings between us. We were just good and began to do what we did best, got on with our lives. Everyone noticed and asked him, "Are you and the hairdresser going out again?" This was how it was always said, and we would end up laughing until we couldn't laugh anymore. Carlos was used to me studying. When I told him I was furthering my career in counselling. "If you want to do that darling, go for it, if it makes you feel happy." He always encouraged me and supported me with anything I wanted to do. That is why I loved him so. We were a couple again and it was no one's business but our own. We used to go out and get the stares and we could see their minds working overtime. Wow! Are they going out with each other again?"

After finishing the level 4, I applied for the degree course in Counselling and Psychotherapy at University and was accepted. I remember my first day. I had been to university before and acquired a degree in Teaching Adults in Further Education. My group seemed to be friendly. We were given an information pack for the course and the instructions for the university.

I was very happy when I was accepted and could pursue my dreams and become the best I could be. It took me a year. It was hard but I handed in some work which I felt was my best. Only to find I had dyslexia. All those times of studying more than everyone else, feeling I'm not as clever as everyone. My tutor Luke made an appointment because he told me that if he hadn't heard me speak in class, he would have failed me. He said, "when I read your work I thought something is wrong here. So, I took it to the dyslexia department and they told me your dyslexic."

"I panicked when you told me you wanted to speak to me. I thought, *have I failed?* Oh, thank you so much, Luke, thank you so much."

"Oh, that's fine. Just go to the dyslexia department tomorrow. They have all your details."

"Thank you again." I went to the dyslexia department and had a test. I had it bad. I now knew that for all these tests that I worked hard to pass, I had to work three times as hard. God, you have done it again.

I passed my course and at the graduation, Luke told me, "Out of all the students, you really deserve this certificate."

"Thank you for helping me and not dismissing me. You are a great tutor". We both laughed as I walked on the stage to receive my certificate. I could hear Marsha and Crystal shouting, and everyone clapping. This was a fantastic day. God, you have done it again. I was fifty years of age.

I was so happy to finish my degree course. I began to be me again. I was with the man who always made me happy and knew me inside and out. Carlos had a daughter the same age as Sabrina from his previous partner. What I loved about Carlos was that he cared for his children and his mum and his stepdad. He made sure his mum's and stepdads shopping was always done every week and he visited them frequently. These are the traits I loved about him. He was considerate, kind and very helpful. He wasn't a fool or a pushover, despite what others may have believed; he was quiet but highly intelligent man. I knew him and he knew me. We both knew our limits with each other and didn't ever want to cross the line.

I had a surprise; it was a limousine. Inside it was very spacious with posh carpet and leather seats with a lot of legroom. The lighting was just right all around. There was nice music that caused us to reminisce, which brought back a lot of memories. The glasses had a bend resembling the letter "S" and had ice inside. We had some drinks and offered a toast to me, the birthday girl. Carlos sat next to me and Violet, my friend for years (after some time she met her partner Saul and got married) sat with her partner. We continue having sips of our drinks. We were driven into town and around town, then driven to the venue. It was great, I enjoyed the experience. Thank you, Marsha, for being so thoughtful and generous.

At the venue, the lighting was perfect, not too much light but not too dark either. The tables were round. The dancefloor was a good size and was wooden and polished. I received a warm welcome with applause as I entered. I invited the people who I knew would love to come and celebrate my birthday with me. It was a great night.

Marsha sang Tina Turner songs; all dressed in glitter. She was marvellous and blew us away with her talent. When she sang *Simply the Best* I cried because it's one of my favourite songs. We danced and enjoyed ourselves that night. The food was very good; the venue was excellent. The only thing was that the parking was difficult for drivers. Everyone had a great night and really enjoyed themselves.

The atmosphere was easy and relaxed. Everyone got on with each other, even though some people only got to know each other that evening. The music was mixed, to cater to everyone. People were invited to say a speech if they wanted to.

I was called to go on the stage. I left Carlos standing next to me. When I went on the stage, I couldn't see him or Ava. I thought he might have gone to the toilet and would come back. Everyone was looking for Carlos to say something. There was no sign of him or Ava.

When I came off the stage Ava said, "I'm sorry for not saying a speech but I can't do it."

Carlos said, "I'm sorry darling, but if I say a speech, call an ambulance for me tonight. I can't do it, sorry, darling." I looked at both of them and started laughing.

The floor was open for us all to dance the night away. Carlos could really dance. Sometimes it felt like there were only us in the room. He would always find something to make me laugh. Sometimes I had to stop because my stomach would hurt me with laughter.

Everyone enjoyed themselves and I really enjoyed it. We got home that night and we all talked about the event and spoke of how the night went. We had a very good sleep, which would mean we wouldn't be up early the next day.

Carlos and I were very happy, when we went out, it felt like it was just the two of us in the building, I remember a guy that we knew, came over and said" What are you two laughing at all the time over here?"

We looked at each other and I said, "Nothing, it's just what Carlos said to me," and we started laughing again. It came naturally and this was our norm. People used to look at us and stare because they saw us so happy. Carlos loved to cook. He was brilliant at it. He would cook most of the time due to me working and studying. He loved to try different dishes. Looking back now, he should have been a chef. When the grandchildren came to the house, he would ask them, "What do you all fancy eating today?" Nothing was a bother. We shared the food shopping but I would add more, as it was only fair. I never took him for granted, neither did he. We were honest with each other.

Carlos had a quiet side to him, too. He was serious when he had to be. If anyone upset him, he would just be quiet and say nothing. I knew when I said something that he didn't like. I could see him watching the TV but he was thinking about what I said. I used to go over to him and say, "I didn't mean to say that or it came out wrong babes, I'm sorry." If I felt he was a bit off, I would say, "What's wrong babes?"

He would say, "Nothing, I'm just watching TV." but I could sense if he was upset. He wasn't one for shouting and arguing, he would stay quiet. I witnessed him really upset once. He walked out of the house and I called him back. He said I'm coming but he didn't come back straight away. I was so upset that he was upset. I opened the door to leave, only to have him walk in. We spoke and we told each other, this will never happen again and it never did.

We were happy for many years. Our fights were brief; our unwillingness to hurt each other always led to quick reconciliations. We both stuck to what we said to each other. We wouldn't hurt one another. We would always find a way to turn things around. We had a special love. We prayed together all the time. We were honest with each other. He was a pleasant man with a good heart. He didn't trouble anyone. If there was an argument, he would walk away not because he was a coward, he preferred peace.

We spoke about anything and everything. We went out when we wished and had all the family at home every Sunday. This was where we all got together. Carlos and I would cook and tidy up. We were a team. If we went out on Saturday, the food would be prepared before going out so we could get up and put the meat and chicken to cook on a slow heat. Then finish everything without rushing or getting up too early.

22.
BECOMING A REGISTERED CENTRE

I still had my business and was still very busy. Pauline, one of my longtime clients, introduced me to Kathy, who was looking for someone to share the building with her. I had a meeting with Kathy and she came across as genuine. She had already set up her training centre to teach individuals how to acquire English qualifications. After meeting her a few times, she told me I could become a training centre too and train others to become hairdressers. Her idea was to assist and help me achieve the registration for the learning centre. I felt that was a challenge and became excited about it. Having received my counselling certificate, I was qualified to teach introductory counselling courses. I'd already earned my Tutor Award for adult education and my Assessor Award.

I knew I had the qualifications to teach hairdressing with the longtime knowledge beneath my belt. This was one of my dreams, to help others to become good hairdressers, as I had learnt from the best. I discussed it with Carlos, the girls, and friends. They said if I felt I wanted to do it, go for it. At this time Sabrina was in college learning hairdressing. I felt this would be a good achievement for her. I could teach her also to achieve her goal. Carlos told me, "As long as you have really thought about it, because this will be a lot of work, and you will have to get staff." I knew this would be very challenging, but I trusted God to help me with this project. Carlos said, "as long as you have a contract between Kathy and yourself, it should be ok." It was important for me to have Carlos's thoughts and suggestions. Kathy and I signed a contract.

Meantime while waiting for the equipment. Kathy and I met frequently to prepare the Rules and regulations for the hairdressing salon. She was very keen to help me by showing me her folder with the legislation that she had for her business. I got my file together and could understand the legislation that I needed for my business.

The salon was downstairs and I would share one of the classrooms upstairs for the students' lectures. The time came, I arranged for the electrician that was recommended previously to do the work. Lucas's work was very good, he was good at his job, and I was very pleased. The furniture was black, silver with white walls, and the towels were red, yellow, black and blue. Each station had a mirror on either side. The chairs were black with silver hand rests. Clients waiting at the reception desk could sit on a matching black leather seat while looking through hair magazines on a silver rack; the desk itself was oval-shaped and made of black leather.

The washing basins were on the far side of the room. The floor had a light grey covering so the floor could be swept and mopped each day. Everything was ready. I blessed the salon asking God to be in this place, making it peaceful and that everyone that came in would have a wonderful experience.

I opened the salon and was busy with clients. Within a few months. I still needed Kathy's help regarding information with the policies, but found her support was not forthcoming. I then realised that there was a slight change. I didn't look too much into it as I thought she was very busy and so was I. I continued to get my rules and regulations in order. It was taking me sometime but I was getting there. I asked for help and I got the support I needed. I continued to do my research and continued, knowing and trusting it would happen.

There were grants being given to companies. Paul was recommended to me, as he had helped this person with his business. I rang Paul and we arranged a meeting. He came across as a very honest, calm natured person. At the end of our meeting, he told me he would be glad to work with me. I was over the moon. I was giving thanks as I needed extra income to develop the business and to keep going. I didn't have any students at this time. The idea was to open an agency for people to have free counselling sessions. I had previously requested a church minister's help in providing a room for my student counsellors a couple of days a week. These were trainees at the end of their courses, as they needed their hours of practical counselling to complete the course. I knew how daunting it was to find clients, because of the lack of spaces in agencies, from my experience of finishing my diploma course in counselling.

I interviewed the students first to find out how they would work with the clients. Then I got them together and assessed them as they practised their skills on each other. Then I would advertise for the clients and match the clients with a student counsellor. The agency worked very well and the students gained their hours and the clients could get the help they needed. I also taught some groups the Introduction to Counselling. These individuals were interested because it allowed them to use the skills at work and gain the skills for their own lives. The groups were also pleased with the course. (I had to make sure they understood they were not qualified counsellors.)

Meantime, Sabrina discovered she was pregnant. She was 19 yrs old. Even though I was concerned for her, I encouraged her to have her baby. We knew nothing about the father of the baby. All we were bothered about was her wellbeing. I had to make sure she was ok. This is life and we have to deal with circumstances as they come. I tried my best to give her all the support I could. She was still at home with me and I cared for her until she had her first son and I had my second grandson, Lucas.

I was there at the birth. When I held Lucas, he pooed on my white uniform (someone told me this meant he was connected to me). Lucas didn't do this to his father. I couldn't believe that my little Sabrina was now a mother. She was a wonderful mother and was so proud. She then got her house; We all helped her as she continued to look after her child. I continued with the salon and eventually my salon was registered as a centre. I gave God thanks. Before long, I had three students. They were enthusiastic to learn. The challenge was ensuring everyone followed their training, which proved difficult. I managed and felt they soon got the skills and were pleased with the results.

The External Verifier visited the salon and asked the students questions regarding their work. They were very vigilant and retained their knowledge and skills. I had an excellent report every time. This made me feel happy and satisfied that I was giving back to others. As time went on, the training centre was doing very well. Clients were coming into the salon and the students could work on their hair with me observing them. Now that I had a registered centre, using upstairs became very difficult. Kathy was acting strangely and not wanting to speak to me. I just couldn't understand that kind of behaviour. I would say hello but she would ignore me and pretend she didn't see me.

I'd just had enough. One day I went into her office and spoke to her. I asked her what was going on. In the contract, we agreed to share the space upstairs. "You allow your students to make so much noise and I've said nothing." I asked her, "What have I done for you to be acting this way?", she said nothing. Then her partner Edward pointed his finger in my face and I told him, "If you point your finger any closer to my face, Edward, there will be trouble today." He quickly put his finger down from my face, as he knew I wasn't joking with him. I'd absolutely had enough of their foolishness. I turned and looked at Kathy, noticed she always touched her nose when she was embarrassed or nervous. I then turned and walked out of her office. I then decided to look for another place. God was so good to me. I got a place in town for six months. I wanted to get the students to pass their course, then think about what I would do next. Sabrina worked with me for a few days. I didn't like where I was. I found them to be prejudiced.

One day, whilst Sabrina was working in the salon, one of the security guards asked, "Why did you come here in the centre? Why didn't you set up your business in the market that we have?" Implying that we didn't belong in the centre.

Sabrina replied confidently, "because we wanted to be here!" Then he left. One day I was doing someone's hair. There were two security guards. One began holding this young man was Caucasian. They had him pinned to the floor, with his knee on his neck. I was so shocked I went out and told them, "This is someone's child. What are you doing?". They continued; I just couldn't watch as I was so upset.

I'm paying for this space and I don't have to witness abuse as well. Another incident happened, whilst I was washing a relaxer out of my client's hair. This big centre had a water problem and the water went off for half an hour. I had to get one of my staff to quickly get some water. By the time I got the chemical off my client's head, there were abrasions on her scalp. Obviously, I was upset for my client and offered treatments. She didn't return. Following this, I contacted my insurers to explain my full agreement with the client's complaint. My insurers agreed, and the client received compensation.

I then decided to leave when my lease finished. My students had passed their courses. My six-month lease was up. I came back home and continued my business as usual. It was a great experience but I knew God would have another place or journey for me.

Kathy from the old business centre called me up one day and asked me to give her the code for the space I used to rent from her. I really wanted to say, "How dare you, asked me anything after you treated me so badly!" I felt a feeling of compassion and a voice saying, "Just tell her." So, I gave her the code and she thanked me before leaving.

Many years later I saw her and she didn't look very well. I looked at her and she turned her head. I've also seen her partner, although someone told me they aren't together anymore. I saw him in the gym, and in a shop some weeks later. He didn't give me any eye contact and pretended he didn't see me. Another time I went into the chemist and he was coming out of the examination room, I said hello and he answered back. I sensed he was embarrassed as he put his coat on. I then went to the counter then left. It's not worth being unkind and nasty, life is too short.

After gaining my Degree as a Psychotherapist, I got a job as a Tutor teaching Counselling for an organisation. I had three classes per week, with

14 students in each class. The Introduction to Counselling was for 10 weeks. I would have about four groups for the year. These individuals would apply for the Level 2 Counselling group, which would be with me for one year. (and I had two groups for one year). There was a lot of preparing, teaching and marking.

Even though I really enjoyed my job. It was stressful. The students had their own issues that I would have to oversee. There were none of my students that didn't pass the courses, as I would give them the support they all needed at different times. I was dedicated and passionate about my job and the students.

There were many nights Carlos sat up with me on a Saturday because I had so much marking to do. He would fall asleep but wouldn't leave me downstairs. He was the kindest person I have ever known to be so caring and understanding. He totally had so much patience with me. I couldn't go out so much, I was so busy and dedicated to the work. He knew this and didn't want to make me feel bad or show me any resentment. Most of the time he said, "It's ok Vee, I don't mind babes, do what you have to do, darling." I made sure we went out sometimes, as I needed to be fair and consider Carlos. He got so used to staying in, it felt like an effort sometimes to get ready. We used to laugh about it, because when we went out we had such a great time.

23.
LOVE AND CARE

One night Carlos didn't feel very well. I called the ambulance. They came quickly and he was admitted into hospital. He had to rest. We were all around him. It felt strange because he was never sick. Looking at him and glancing at the girls, their faces, they told a story of sadness, worry, and they were close to tears. He had to have a pacemaker fitted. Carlos didn't want anyone to know. He didn't want to look weak. I told him it's nothing to be ashamed of. Things happen in life that we can't do anything about.

No one knew about this except the girls. This was his wish. We always prayed before any doctor's or hospital appointment. Carlos looked after me and it was a pleasure to be by his side. The only people knew were the girls because they came around every Sunday. I had to be very strict with him.

He would say, "I'm ok now." I made sure he rested and I kept an eye on him.

I would ask, "How are you feeling?" He would reply, "I'm feeling a lot better," but I could tell by his voice he wasn't, really. He just didn't want me to worry. I went to every appointment with him.

I wanted nothing to go wrong with my darling. He was my life. I wanted him to be well. Looking at him, I think he knew what I was thinking. This is a west Indian saying meaning What girl What do you want now.

I would go over to him and kiss his handsome face and neck. He used to laugh and say you're tickling me; he was very ticklish.

Gradually, he was sorted and returned to his old self. He began to take care of himself by making sure he took his medication regularly, by doing light exercises, eating healthily and monitoring his intake. I was very proud of him. Recovering, he cooked. Our taste-offs spurred us on, and we grew closer. We went nowhere without each other. We laughed everywhere we went. We enjoyed each other's company. We then went to the West Indies and I made all the bookings and Carlos told his family in the West Indies we were coming to visit. They were very excited and couldn't wait to see us.

Carlos and I went to the Caribbean for four weeks. We stayed with his late brothers' children. We enjoyed it so much. As Carlos had a pacemaker fitted, I made sure he was ok throughout the flight. It was great, just the two of us. The family was very welcoming. Carlos's sister-in-law Florence and his niece Estella, nephews Calvin, and Max had already been to the UK when Carlos's dear mum passed.

They stayed with us and we made sure they enjoyed their stay. When they came over, I had the training academy and I was very busy so they had the house to themselves. We showed them how to get the bus and to get to town and get back home. They were over the moon. When I got in, they would leave me some dinner, which was really nice. This was how the relationship grew between me and his family in the West Indies. As far as I was concerned, we were all one. (Carlos's family and my family are all one). We weren't married on paper but in our hearts we were. He loved me and I loved him for us. That was all that mattered.

Carlos's Sister-in-law Florence and her daughter Estella. They were in the UK for four weeks and visited Carlos's mum in the residential home. We all used to visit her frequently, every two days. I used to call her Mum. She was a beautiful soul with a heart of gold. Mum was always very nice towards me and made me feel welcome when I went to her and her partner

Nolan' home. I went on my own several times. Mum was very friendly. This is where Carlos gets it from.

When Mum passed, I went with Carlos to see her. He was obviously broken. This was the first time I saw Carlos cry. We were both crying for some time. I didn't know what to do but to let him cry for his Mum. I felt so helpless but knew how it felt; it brought back memories of my Mum's death. The pain was excruciating, without a doubt.

It was some weeks before either of us could laugh or smile. Carols loved his mum so she was his life. It was hard seeing Carlos so lost and broken. I just held him at night and reassure him Mum was with him and around him. I was also watching closely as I knew He was not too well either. It was a very hard time for him and I made sure I looked after my Carlos as best as I could.

Death is so hard and sad when we have to say goodbye to the ones we love and treasure dearly. Carlos asked me if I would help him with Mum's funeral. "Of course, I will. She was my Mum too." I really loved Mum's spirit. She was a very kind and fair person. This made me love Carlos even more. I told Mum one time, "Thank you mum for bringing up such a lovely man for me to have." she started smiling. Talking to Mum reminded me of my Mum. She wasn't bothered, "if Carlos did something that was wrong," she would say, "he's wrong and not cover up for him. When Carlos was younger, a girl knocked on the door and his mom asked if she knew he had a girlfriend. The girl said, "No he didn't tell me that". The girl left. Mum told Carlos don't mess people about it's not fair. That is why I loved her so much. She was very honest and I have always agreed with that. Don't do unto other what you don't want them to do to you. My mother used to say you can't be wrong and strong.

Carlos's Neice and two of his nephews came up for Mum's funeral. They stayed for two weeks with us.

A few years later, we went to the Caribbean. We were in love, happy, and free to do what we wanted to do. The hot sun beating down with a lovely breeze. As we walked toward the town, the scenery was amazing. Carlos's family lived 10 minutes away near the sea, in the distance where the locals were selling drinks, fruits, and food. It's about a different life. I felt so free and loved, with Carlos by my side. As usual, he had me laughing and begging him to stop with the jokes. We walked by the sea, and watched the waves and people on the beach, just sitting and enjoying the view. After two hours we went back home and cooked before Carlos's family got home.

The house smelt of the delicious aroma from those pots, which caused me to feel really hungry. Together, we would wash up and tidy up. Then we would go out on the veranda to watch people walk by. I loved being in the sun but Carlos always was in the shade. After Carlos' niece, Jasmin, and his nephew, Owen appeared in the doorway. "Good afternoon, Uncle, and Aunty. How was your day?"

"Good afternoon." We both replied and continued speaking to both of them. We went down to the bay front for a few hours. We looked around and came back. We ate, washed up and went to sit out on the veranda, to watch everyone passing and get as much sun as possible whilst Carlos stayed in the shade.

The next day we travelled to the other island to visit my family. It was a beautiful day, sunny and hot. The sea was calm, with a wonderful sea breeze. It made me think of how many times my Mum told me about her travels between both islands to visit family and friends. The good times she had in the holiday seasons. A smile would appear on her face, which lit up the room with the joy of the carnival and carnival masquerade.

I remember my father's costume and the dancers' whips at my first carnival; it was scary, and I'm still undecided about it. I was also in the carnival dressed as a Mexican girl; I was sixteen. It brought so many memories of that day. It was the first time I was in a troop. I was very shy and disliked being the centre of attraction. It helped me to be brave and not to be so shy. I saw it again on Yorkshire TV 2024 after the carnival that year. Watching the brief clip showed me how young and unsure I felt about myself.

When we arrived on the Island of my birth, it gave me a sense of belonging. The sun was beating down as we stood for a bus to get to my auntie's house. Carlos and I went to see my Aunty Virginia. This was the first time she'd seen Carlos. I told my Aunty Virginia how sad I felt when

I heard of the passing of my Aunty Evie. She was a wonderful person, full of life, joyful, and very kind.

My other cousin Sophie lived with my Aunty now. It was so good to see her. We hadn't seen each other since Sophie was a teenager; she was grown up now. She was tall and slim, with large brown eyes, an oval-shaped face, with a broad smile showing her lovely white teeth and her hair wonderfully braided. Very well spoken, with a humble soft tone to her voice. We began exchanging our views on the difference between the UK and the Caribbean. Sophie had an excellent job and was happy in the Caribbean and didn't fancy the cold weather in the UK.

They served us dinner; time flew, and soon it was time to leave. It was great seeing my aunty Virginia and Sophie. We walked around the back garden and then hugged each other, said our goodbyes. The bus was coming in the distance and we got on the bus and waved until everyone was out of sight. We had a great time and it was so good to see family.

We then walked back to get the boat to the other island. The sun was shining so brightly; it was very hot but had a lovely breeze. Then the boat came and we boarded it. The boat was not full but had comfortable seats. The fresh air and sea breeze was delightful to feel. And the views of the island were beautiful. I felt a part of me was sad to leave this wonderful paradise again without knowing when I would be back. The boat trip was sensational, and romantic, with Carlos by my side. We looked at each other several times and smiled. This was our holiday, our time, to do whatever we needed to do. As I looked at Carlos, I could feel his love just by him looking at me. This love was for real. Any time he touched me, I felt this feeling of acceptance, belonging and, above all, a wonderful sensation within my being. I loved his light brown eyes. When he looked at me, I just felt this feeling of joy and love. This was my soft spot for him.

After 20 minutes of being on this wonderful boat, we arrived on the Island we left this morning. We went to Carlos's family home. We arrived to see his nephew and niece at home. Carlos heads for the kitchen. I joined him within 10 minutes to help with dinner. Soon all the food was prepared and was cooking. As usual, Carlos's pot is now boiling and you can smell the aroma within the house. Carlos shouts, "dinner will not be long!" I started laughing, as I knew he enjoyed cooking. I went back into the kitchen to see if there was anything I could do. The answer was," it's ok darling, just rest. I'm almost finished now."

I didn't want him to do too much so I sat down in the Kitchen and asked him, "are you ok? Is there anything you want me to do?"

"No darling, everything is almost done."

"Ok babes."

Carlos's niece Jasmin came in from work, followed by his nephew Owen. "Good afternoon everyone. Oh, I can smell the pot, Uncle Carlos."

"Yes, it's nearly ready, Jasmin." We all laughed.

Owen asked, what are you cooking today, Uncle?"

"Oh, we having sweet potatoes, yam, dumplings, planting, and fish."

"Oh, that will be nice, Uncle," said Owen and I agreed. All four of us had dinner together, which was absolutely delicious. We all thanked Carlos for the wonderful dinner, then I washed up and Carlos and I went on the veranda to enjoy the warm weather. Jasmin and Owen went to their bedrooms to rest.

Our holiday was ending. We started thinking what we should buy everyone. The decision was to shop the next day, so we could take our time without rushing. We went to bed earlier than usual.

Waking up to warmth and sunshine was a wonderful thing. I felt so free and really happy. We shopped today for gifts for everyone. After writing our list and having breakfast, then having our shower, we were ready for the day. We went into town. Everyone knew we were from abroad and would greet us and knew the family we were staying with.

Walking around had to be done slowly. As the sun was beating down, we had to stop for a drink and shelter from the sun. We decided to go home earlier than planned and get the other gifts the next day. We were on our own at home and decided to have a shower and have an afternoon nap. This was a great idea. We were exhausted. Carlos didn't have to cook; he did enough food for two days. At 5:30 PM, we headed to the beach, alive with music and open bars. Everyone would meet for a few hours to socialise and have drinks.

Alexis accompanied us. He was another nephew of Carlos's. Alexis was tall, very dark-skinned, with dreadlocks and a lovely smile. He was dressed in his short and a nice tee shirt. He was very polite and handsome. He had a straight nose, just like Carlos. If I didn't know, I would have thought he was Carlos's son. I met him earlier for a short while when we arrived. He said he would try and meet us depending on what time he finished work. We had a great time dancing and singing to the songs, whilst the sound of the sea's crashing waves kissed the sand in the background. I can remember this sound, and a calm feeling takes over me from this beautiful island of paradise. I had to close my eyes and tell myself *I am home*. Alexis walked us home and headed home because he had work the next day. We thanked him for his kindness and hugged him before going.

The next day we laid in bed sharing the experience and the good time we were having. We prayed and thanked God for safety, good health, and protection. We hugged, kissed and told each other how we loved each other. We lay in each other's arms for a while before getting up. Everything felt so perfect. I had the love of my life who loved me back.

Eventually we got up, had breakfast, a shower and got ready to shop for the rest of the gifts. The town was very busy. We went to the bank, the was a long queue. I had to change some money into the Eastern Caribbean Dollar. Carlos sat while I waited in the queue. It took about 15minutes. We then continued finished the gift shopping. This was great to know we were free again to concentrate on the rest of our holiday, which was just four days.

We had already planned for my cousin to pick us up and take us both to his home tomorrow. We would stay for two days. I could see my family before I left the Island. They lived 10 minutes away from Carlos's family home. We cooked before Jasmin and Owen got home. Dinner was lamb with rice, carrots, peas, and potatoes. Carlos peeled the potatoes and veg. I cleaned the lamb, seasoned it with a blend of spices, and left it to cook.

While the dinner was cooking, we talked about how we'd spent our day. We asked how work was for both of them. Soon dinner was ready and we all sat around the table, as the kitchen was very spacious. We ate and chatted amongst ourselves; I felt this was a special time for us to talk about our lives and what was going on for us, individually., Within this short time, we learnt a lot about each other's work, lifestyle and how we felt about things that bothered us. I felt this enlightened us to know each other more.

We reminded them we would be away for two days. I was looking forward to seeing Tristin, who was hilarious and would have you laughing at his silly jokes. We washed up and headed to the veranda to enjoy the sun and breeze and watch everyone passing by. We had a wonderful view of the house. Houses lined the alley; its far end opened onto the main road, near the local shop. People passing and cars driving by. We went to bed a bit earlier tonight, as we planned to go to the beach for a walk and sit and have a drink by the stalls and listen to music.

Today I awoke with the scorching sun beating down and the birds tweeting. I looked across at Carlos, who was still sleeping. I lay there watching him sleep. I was in love with this man. His round face, his natural dark black eyebrows, his straight nose, and shapely groomed moustache and well-shaped beard. He looked so handsome even when he slept. He looked so peaceful and comfortable.

I'd usually watch him in the morning until he woke up, then I sometimes closed my eyes to see what he would do. He'd always hug me close, nuzzling my head. I would snuggle up against him to feel his loving body around mine. He was very special to me and I told him all the time.

He allowed me to be myself and I also allowed him to be himself. By his actions, I knew he adored me. He would be upset if anyone was awful or hurt me in any way. Everywhere we went, people would admire us. They would tell me how good we looked together and how we looked so happy and we were very happy. He was my darling, my special person who I would do anything for. No one could say anything bad about him as if they did, I wouldn't have anything to do with them. He was my good or bad apple, as my mother used to say about me. The love is real and no one could take that from us. No one. Only God can separate us.

This morning, Carlos opened his eyes and said, "How long have you been awake, babes?"

"Not long darling." I replied

"Come here babes, are you ok?" he said, putting his hand around me. "Did you have a good sleep, darling?"

"Yes darling, I did," I replied.

"What time did you want to go out?" Asked Carlos,

"What time do you think we should go out? Are you still tired, babes?" I asked

"No, I'm ok, we can go when you're ready." Carlos replied.

We prayed to God giving thanks for Him protecting our families, friends, and everyone who didn't know him. We thanked him for the life he has given us.

We eventually got up to another wonderful day of sunshine, blue sky, and this lovely island of paradise. We made breakfast, showered, dressed, and were ready for the day. As we walked, we started speaking about the Island and Carlos's life growing up. He mentioned going to the beach with his friends, how they taught each other to swim, by throwing each other in to the sea. How they used to catch fish, by dangling strong strings with worms on the end into the sea and sit still for hours.

As he spoke, I could see his face light up with excitement, looking at the sea and smiling. They were the days we had little, but what we had was a good life. As we walked, there was a sense of walking down the road Carlos walked, looking through his eyes, the time of immense joy and happiness within the community, because everyone was striving for the same thing, to make their world better.

There were people sitting on the beach, just taking in the scenery. The sea was far out. The locals were sitting and enjoying the breeze, wearing hats that sheltered them from the sun.

As we walked the side road, cars, and buses transported people back and forth. I was thrilled to feel the sun on my back. There was a feeling of peace and tranquillity. Watching the sea and feeling the warm breeze meant so much to me. This feeling of being on the Island at this very moment gave me such an overwhelming feeling of belonging.

When we got to the beach where the stalls were, Carlos bought us drinks. We sat down on a bench and enjoyed the music. "This is the life," I said to Carlos.

He smiled, "I know, it's great." We were watching people go by. Women lugged large bags, clearly from the market. Some women were well dressed, men with ties looked like they worked in offices. I wondered how they kept a tie on in this hot weather. As the sun got hotter, I looked at Carlos, who had already run for cover. I smiled. I felt he knew what I was going to say and do. "Are you hot enough, babes?" He shouted to me.,

"Yes, I am babes. I will join you now." I got up and went under the shelter, which was provided. "Oh, that's better babes, suddenly I got so hot. Wow!"

On our way home, the locals were under trees and sheltering from the sun. I thought if they are doing it, then we have to do it too. After getting to a shop, I asked Carlos to let us stay in the shade for a few minutes and have a cool drink, which we did. After a while, people started leaving the shop and so did we. The sun had cooled down, so we continued getting home. When we got in the house, we were so happy for the cool atmosphere. We stripped down, took a refreshing shower, and dozed off until it was time to prepare for my cousin Tristin to pick us up.

Seeing Tristin was great. He had come to the UK and stayed with me for a month before going back home. I made sure his stay was enjoyable. I knew he wanted me to come to his house so he could look after us. He told me he's not a cook, so we picked up some things to cook for the Two days we were there. We enjoyed our stay. I knew most of his friends from the last time I met him. It was good seeing them again. After dinner, we all talked and drank. There was a lot of laughter and jokes. We all spoke about what had happened in our lives since we last met. We had a great time at Tristin's. He then took us back to Carlos's cousins the next evening and wished us a safe journey home to the UK and left.

When it was time to return to the UK, Jasmin saw us off. We thanked them for their hospitality and allowing us to stay with them throughout our holiday. When we came back from our holiday. We were greeted by everyone. My three wonderful daughters. My beautiful and handsome grandchildren were all here to welcome us home. Music and balloons greeted our taxi's arrival.

This was such a lovely welcome by my daughters and grandchildren. I felt so special. Looking back at Carlos, he was also overwhelmed. This was so wonderful. I really felt blessed. I came back to a decorated home, which Marsha did most of the work but was accompanied by Sabrina and Crystal. It felt so nice. The entrance, the dining room, back room, and the kitchen were immaculate.

Walking up the stairs was amazing. It was freshly painted; the bathroom was lovely with matching mats and towels. With small plants. My bedroom was breathtaking. The walls had a cream paper which matched the ceiling. There were two enormous pictures. One on the wall as you came through the door, on the left. This picture had four trees and the biggest tree covered the other trees with a show which glistens as I moved my head. The tree in the middle is the dominant feature. Its branches, full of snow, covered the other trees, blending in with them to create the appearance of one beautiful tree. The glitter is sprinkled to give an appearance of snow glistening, which causes the picture to become so real. As I keep looking at it looks like it coming towards me which makes it look like it's coming alive.

The other picture with a ballerina with feather as a costume bending her head down between her folded arms was next to the window and near to a large mirror, on the right. The dresser is nearly the length of the wall. The covering was white before. My TV is on the left-hand side. I have my mum and dad's photo, my makeup, all my creams for my face and body, and perfumes. The dresser was now a gold colour. It looked stunning and still does.

The rest of the house was pristine and fresh. The incense filled the air with a fragrant aroma.

The home makeover, particularly our bedroom, astonished and delighted Carlos and I. Financially, my daughters did a great job. It was astounding. I cherished my daughters for their caring hearts and the love they show me. Everyone was at the house that afternoon. It was great to see the grandchildren. They all seemed to have grown a few inches. I missed them so much. I kissed and hugged my daughters and grandchildren. In my heart, I gave God thanks for taking Carlos and me to the Caribbean and back home to our family.

We all continued meeting as usual on Sundays. Sabrina's three children, two boys and a girl, would get dropped off on Friday and go home Sunday for school the next day, from two weeks old. I also had Crystal's girl and son when they were born. They all stayed with me from two weeks old to give my daughter a rest. Marsha and her daughter lived with me.

My grandchildren and Crystal visit Friday through Sunday, heading home before the work/school week starts. Marsha and her daughter are always present because they live with me. Twelve of us typically gather, with family potentially joining later. Before dinner Carlos and I would pray, then someone would read a chapter from the bible. We would talk about what it meant to each of us to get a better understanding. We would then speak about our week if anything had happened that we wanted to share. This is the time most of the stories come out and there may be laughter and questions or just have no words because everyone is so taken back with laughter. Then the dinner would be shared out, we would eat, then the music would be turned on and we would end up dancing. This was our Sundays which kept us together for so many years.

Crystal's two children used to stay with me. Until they were grown and even now the granddaughter still sleepover. Sabrina's children would also stay at the house each Friday to Sunday, from the age of two weeks. Their presence brought joy. I looked after them with my life. We would pray, read the bible and I would explain the word of God and tell them about the Creator. "Train up a child in the way he should go even when he is old he will not depart from it." Proverbs 22:6 (ESV) 2016. I have done this with my girls and now my grandchildren. I'm not stating I'm perfect but I have been taught by my mother and grandmother, who was wise. Without their input, I would not be the person I am today.

Our Christmases and New Years were great. Everyone contributed. Carlos and I did the meat, turkey, and fish and rice and peas. Crystal would do the coleslaw, roast potatoes, macaroni, mix vegetables, and her special dumplings. Once you've tasted these dumplings, you have to fight yourself to stop eating them. Marsha would decorate the house and clean. Sabrina would make the salad. Everyone would bring a bottle to contribute. This was our time to celebrate with each other and keep the family together. We did this for years.

24

THE CHANGE

As time went by, our love was always there. We cared and supported each other always, no matter what. I was working as usual but became very committed to teaching counselling skills. I had now been working for four and a half years at this company. I felt it was time to consider whether I should stay or leave. At the end of term, my students would usually give me gifts and lots of flowers. So many gifts and flowers from one class last term I needed help to carry them. As we were entering my room, the director and manager had to stand to one side to allow the four students to pass. And wait until I had opened the office door. I felt a change in the atmosphere. My mind sensed that they didn't really like it but it wasn't my fault if the students wanted to give me gifts. The courses were finished, with all of my students passing the course. For the next semester, I got a letter stating that my classes have been reduced because of funding. I had three classes each week and it would be reduced to two. I said yes, because I loved teaching.

I received another letter stating I had to have a meeting with a manager and she wanted to see me before I started teaching that evening. We agreed to meet one hour and a half before my lessons started. I had to make sure I had enough time to do some printing and also had some time for myself before teaching. The meeting was about one of my students that had just passed in time before the term ended. Six weeks into the course, her portfolio lacked explanations for several questions.

I opposed her late start; it would cause her to fall behind and miss group bonding. The manager insisted on letting her enrol on the course. So, I said, "If this person can catch up, that's fine but she has to do a lot of work by herself."

When the student came on the course, she felt like a fish out of water, as I thought she would. She found it very difficult at first but was always catching up. The course was intense for her. She usually would ask me a lot of questions in class that she didn't understand. I would try my best to help her. I could explain the question but she had to do her research and do the work. I sometimes wondered if she was planted there for them to get rid of me.

This manager started speaking about this student. I got the impression that she didn't feel that the course was up to standard. She asked me, "Didn't you explain the information clearly for her to understand?" My argument was that within the four years, no one had complained about or reported my style of teaching. I felt my teaching wasn't the issue. I told her what I told my manager before having this student enrolled on the course. She said she understood where I was coming from.

I told her after one hour; I had to do some printing for the class this evening. I went into the staff room only to find everything was packed up and I couldn't find anything that I needed. I had to ask the other staff members to show me where things were. I went to print handbooks, only to find the printer connected to the manager's office. I had to ask for someone to get the handbooks.

Entering the classroom, I found tables and chairs rearranged, not in the usual horseshoe formation for counselling. I asked the waiting manager to rearrange the classroom furniture. She told me I can teach like this. I told her I can't teach a class like this; the tables had to go and chairs needed to be set up the way I liked them. She was red in the face and very bewildered and upset. And called the caretaker to move the tables and she helped him.

I stood still and watched her rushing, taking the tables out of the room and her face and neck became red as beetroot. I would lift nothing because that is not in my job description. Then she told me she would stay and observing this evening. I said "Ok." and she sat down. I prayed in my heart and started by introducing myself to the 18 students in the room, sitting in chairs as a horseshoe. I continued with the class by marking the register and reading the handbook. Then went on to rules as a counsellor, by allowing the class to brainstorm. Time raced; break time was here. I knew the students enjoyed the introduction and the session went very well.

The manager got up and told me she was going now. Then I asked her to give me her feedback on my performance, "How did you feel the session has gone so far?"

"It was ok." she said and left. I knew she wasn't pleased and all that happened this evening was a setup, for me to fail. At the end of the evening, the students were happy and excited to continue the rest of the course. I knew within my heart I wasn't happy with what just happened and started praying for what I had to do. I had to think fast.

As I went back upstairs, it was very clear I would not continue and I packed up all of my books and belongings and knew I would not be back here to teach. It was a very clear and precise feeling I heard that small voice saying, "Leave" this was the last night I would teach here. It was a very sad time for me as this was the same building I was taught by my tutors. The same office I came to see my Tutors if I needed their help or advice. This building was special and the room I taught my students was the same room I was taught in.

The whole building meant a lot to me. Sharing my life story with my class and addressing difficult life issues with others yielded both joy and sorrow. Making myself vulnerable, because I had to be truthful and strong enough to admit when I regretted, wrong doings, admitting my faults, and how I really felt at times within my life. Before I could ever be an effective counsellor, I had to search my heart and my whole being to understand another and to help anyone.

Driving home, I rang Crystal and told her of my decision and why I decided to leave the college. She was very sorry to hear this news. She knew how dear I felt about my students and teaching the course. When I got home, my thoughts became muddled. I asked Crystal to help me write my resignation and she did. I told Marsha, who understood and told me not to worry mum, we will manage, because I still had to pay the mortgage. She reassured me not to worry Mum. I will pay the mortgage; you always tell us God will make a way and he always does.

The next day I got up, showered as usual. Different clothes they haven't seen, makeup, my best perfume, looking very smart. Making sure I looked good. On arrival, I let myself in as normal. I thought as I tapped the numbers to get into the building. *I won't be doing this ever again.* I said hello to everyone I met whilst walking up the two flights of stairs, which took me past my office and looked at the door. I went straight to the manager's office and knocked. I heard, "Come in."

I opened the door and said, "Good morning, I would like to give you this." as I handed her the envelope. I stayed to hear her reply.

As she opened the letter, she said, "I understand." I looked at her and she went red again like a beetroot.

I walked out of her office and closed the door and continued walking down the entrance and saw my colleague. I looked through the glass window of the door, and when she saw me, she came out and said with a big smile on the face. "What are you doing here this early?"

I replied, "I have just resigned." She looked shocked as I told her. "I will tell you about it later", I said. I then gave her my number. She called me later that afternoon and we had a lengthy talk. "I don't know what's going on but nothing is organised."

"There are so much changes going on, Jackie (the manager) came into my class last week, and just said I will assess you this morning without informing me first."

I replied, "Yes, this is the same thing she did to me when I came in yesterday afternoon".

She looked at me with sadness and said, "I will miss you; I can't believe they have treated you so badly." She said.

I told her, "You just look after yourself and don't let these people make you ill. It's not worth it.". As she spoke to me, I could hear in her voice how worried she was because her husband wasn't well and she was the only breadwinner. We rang each other a few times after that, but we got busy and, unfortunately, didn't speak again.

After leaving the training centre, I continued working and building my business in hairdressing. I became very busy. I also was asked by some of my clients if they could have a few counselling sessions. I was very concerned and asked my supervisor for his thoughts and the rules and regulations. I felt the way forward was to tell the clients that the counselling sessions and the hair are similar, but not the same. In the counselling setting, it's all about them and I can't give them my opinions and advice. It would be different, as it's all about their feelings, fears, and issues. I will try to help unfold those parts they find difficult so they can find their way through their feelings.

There were a few clients that found the sessions very useful, as I have the knowledge of using several techniques which assist and allow them to focus on issue's they find complicated to move on with their lives. The counselling skills have helped me so much to understand myself and to enlighten my life. It's very important that when situations, disruptions, and disappointments happen, I usually ask myself, what part did I play in this situation and how can I solve this? If I can't voice the feelings, does it hurt? Am I angry? Why did this happen and recognise the feeling in my body? This is the beginning of recognising. What did I contribute to this situation. Can I talk to that person or not? Sometimes you're not at that place just yet. It can become hard to process but the longer it's not acknowledged, it can start festering to the point of it becoming even more intense. This is a place of hurt, anger, and hate. This can become uncomfortable to the point of feeling unwell, physically.

25.
FORGIVENESS

The organs of the body can't stand such painful conditions. I know in the past what stress and worry feel like, is not how I want to live my life ever. There is a saying life is what you make it (it's so true). Life is great, but issues will always come. But I can overcome it by forgiving others. This helps me to put things into perspective. Forgiving is the most rewarding thing that has allowed me to free myself from illness and sadness. High blood pressure that I developed when I was mistreated at my last job. A tutor who worked there for years was dismissed and mistreated, took them to court and won the case. The price of all this, I ask myself, *is it worth it*? And my answer is, "not at all." My health means more to me than anything.

The most freeing thing I have ever done in my life is to forgive others and forgive myself. It has made me happier, contented, calm and a feeling of acceptance to know I will get things wrong. I am not and will never be perfect. I can say sorry to anyone without feeling small or intimidated. My mother used to say you can't be *wrong and strong*. I now understand that. It's nothing to do with age or feeling that person may have the upper hand or feeling embarrassed about saying sorry. It allows you to be strong and bold to admit I am wrong. Making sure your free of guilt and you're not carrying any strife or bitterness for anyone in your heart. If I feel I can't approach that person, I will pray about it and know that there is a higher power, the creator, who will forgive me. Since I have come to this revelation, I have felt so free from stress and worry. I'm confident in taking charge of my feelings and happiness, and I'm understanding of others.

It has changed my mind set, more than I could ever hope for. People have told me I look younger. I thank God for what he is doing in this life he has given me and freed me to be a happier person. When I look into the mirror, I see a person who has given everything over to God who has answered and changed my heart. I'm now at peace to hold on to Gods unchanging hand. Knowing I am protected and loved by him. God is in control of me, and the life he has given me, for that I am so thankful.

26.
IS LOVE NOT ENOUGH?

Carlos and I continued to be the best we could be. We loved each other but we knew there were certain things that had changed for us and we both found it difficult to cope with. We were, at times, ignoring it, as if it wasn't there. Carlos was very smart and very in tune with everyone around him. I know others would see a man that was very quiet at times, but full of jokes and stories that would make anyone laugh. He may have appeared not to be aware of things that happened around him, but that was so very wrong. He was very clued up, intelligent and very smart. I knew him very well. He would not take nonsense from anyone. He would appear to be cool about things but would eventually leave politely. You wouldn't know if he was upset. You just wouldn't see him for a long time. I loved him because he would say to me, Darling you don't have to tell people, they don't have to tell you, all you do is watch and listen to them. This meant by listening you can have a glimpse of what is going on with this person and by what they are saying without asking a word. He was very wise and pretended he heard no one or nothing. All he wanted was peace and no bad feelings around him. I loved and understood his strategy.

As I write, this is the hardest thing I have to express about the last days.

Continuing the issues that arose for us. We couldn't get past it or work out how to get around it. It was the worst time of our lives. We loved each other but didn't want to hurt each other ever. We decided to leave it there and not to say we had finished but we knew what it was.

"Will you do that thing for me?" he asked me.

I replied, "of course I will." I knew what he meant, if anything happened to him he wanted me to carry out his wishes. This was the worst time of our lives and eventually Carlos spent most of the time in his flat, then covid-19 struck.

I thought about him all the time; we used to meet at the park because it was near both our homes. I looked at him and knew he wouldn't show any discomfort around me. I respected him too much to show feelings that would upset him, because I still loved him and cared for him. Sabrina, her three children, and Marsha and her daughter stayed with me throughout the lockdown.

The times were very hard. Carlos and I had cooling off time allow us to get used to being apart. It was hard for both of us. We had been here before, but this time it was very different and felt worse than ever. I thought about Carlos, and prayed he would be ok, during these times when everyone was so frightened about this pandemic.

Carlos and I phoned each other to make sure everything was ok. This went on until the end of the pandemic. I would always ask Carlos to come to see me and the family. I would invite him over for dinner on Sundays when everyone was around. When they left, we would have a talk just the two of us. As usual, he would make me laugh and he would have me in stitches. It was like nothing ever happened.

One day Carlos called me and told me he had fallen down the stairs in his flat. I was devastated. My heart leaped with shock and I started crying. I shouted Marsha from her bedroom and she didn't hesitate to take him to the hospital. I called several times to see what was going on. He was being checked by the doctor and they were waiting on the results. I continued praying because I knew the steps were steep. I felt so helpless but someone had to stay with the baby.

Eventually, Carlos and Marsha came home. Carlos's face was very swollen and bruised. He said he was going home now. I said, "You're not going anywhere you're staying with me until you're better."

He replied, "Are you sure?"

I said, "You are staying with us." Carlos looked shocked. I said, "Yes darling, you're staying with me."

I wouldn't allow him to go back to his flat alone, with his head and face covered in bruises. He tried to break his fall and damaged his wrist up to his elbow. I cried when I saw my Carlos ill and hurting. While he stayed with me. I did all the cooking; he looked very frail and wasn't himself. I wouldn't and couldn't let him leave. I nursed him, making sure he was comfortable.

It was great having Carlos. Although, he wasn't well most of the time. He had continuous headaches, on his left side, his head, arm, hand and his leg. His head, his side and his face were bruised. I nursed him and made sure he was ok, by making sure he rested. It was a pleasure to look after him, making sure I was doing the very best for him. It broke my heart to see him like this. At times I would cry without him seeing me. I didn't want him to know and get upset.

When the rest of the family heard they came down to see him, as they hadn't seen Carlos like this ever. Everyone hugged him and I could see the joy in his face and his gladness to be in the moment. Despite sharing a bed, our relationship was strictly friendly; we only offered each other companionship. He knew what kind of person I was; I knew he would respect our friendship more than anything.

During the Christmas season, all the family was at the house. We would have prawn cocktail for starters then the main course, which is turkey, lamb, fish, sweet potatoes, white potatoes roasted, peas and rice, plain rice (usually for the children), Yorkshire puddings, Dauphinoise potatoes, mixed vegetables, dumplings and puddings, ice cream, apple pie, and custard and gateau. We usually have a feast. With heads bowed in gratitude, the family blessed the bountiful meal. The clatter of forks and happy chatter filled the room as they ate, later packing containers with enough food to last several days. It was great having Carlos with us again. I loved his company, but he was quiet, that's how I knew he wasn't himself.

He stayed with me for a few more weeks until he felt better and returned to his flat. I then went away for a break and told his daughter to keep an eye on him for me. Even though my girls would do it anyway.

It was about then when I started speaking to a guy who I quite liked. I told Carlos about him, but all he told me was, "Just look after yourself." We remained good friends and I told this man about Carlos and that he would always be in my life. If he was ill and needed me, I would go to his aid. I told him I wasn't a person to do anything behind anyone's back. He said that's ok. I felt Carlos and I had been through so much and he has always been my rock and will be as long as we live.

Months later, I was with this new man and I saw Carlos crossing the road. I called him, as I knew he didn't see me. I introduced this man to Carlos and they touched fists and as Carlos turned away and we started talking, Carlos shouted to me, "Look after yourself!"

"I will." I replied. As I watched Carlos cross the road, I felt his sadness and I started thinking, *Why did he say that?* Carlos was a man that noticed people by their body language and what came out of their months. His comment to me caused me to question myself.

Blake told me he loved me and wanted to marry me. He said I should live with him in another county. I told him I would not be leaving my home to live anywhere else; I'm not a person that jumps for joy when a man says he loves me and wants to marry me. This relationship was very strange. I noticed he liked a drink but it was more than I felt was ok. He had two cataracts removed. It appeared that he had an infection, but because he wanted to drink, he was hesitant of taken the medication. Every day he would have four strong lagers. I felt that this man didn't really care about his health. He was more bothered about drinking. I wasn't used to this life. He would start a conversation and end up arguing if I didn't agree with him. I started thinking about how Carlos and I were. I knew this was a mistake and I started looking at him very differently. What have I got myself into. He didn't think of his health. How could he care about anyone else. His face was covered with scabs, even then he preferred to drink and not take his medication. I wasn't used to this kind of life. I would stay in the bedroom whilst he was in the front room. I thought why am I here in this room when I have a wonderful clean comfortable home. It just didn't make sense.

I realised at the beginning of the relationship., he would buy four lagers very day and occasionally bought me a bottle of southern comfort. I felt he was being considerate but soon realised it was a cover up to hide his habit. When he finished his lagers, he would ask me if he could have some of the drink he bought me. I'm not a big drinker and I decided not to become dependent on drinking every night. I soon realised his drinking problem and confronted him, but he denied it every time, his eyes evading mine. He insisted he didn't have a problem, by missing a day from drinking. He would go back to his original state of arguing. I did give him a few chances as no one is perfect and tried to help him to cut down the lagers. He just couldn't do it. I then knew he was possibly addicted. I had to remove myself from this relationship.

One day we went out to get some shopping only to hear, "I want to wee!" Before we got to his house he peed himself. I felt sorry for him as he headed to the toilet to clean up. He soon opens a tin of lager. I watched him and prayed about this relationship. Sometimes God allows you to be in someone's life to help them to turn to God. I found out he would argue and curse. I knew this was not for me. I had to get him to go peacefully.

One night I had to ask Crystal to come and help to pack and get him out of the house. He was drunk and out of control. I was very upset but asked God to protect us and allow him to go in peace. He said he would get a taxi to where he lived. My daughter helped this to happen. He had to go into a hotel until the next day,

The taxi man called and told us he would be collecting him the next day to take him to his destination. He has tried to say sorry. I told him I forgive him for everything he did to me. I don't want him to contact me or my family, but I wish him all the best in life, but I will not have anything to do with him, ever. I did tell him I will not be disrespected by anyone. God doesn't want us to be fearful or treated badly. We have to care for each other and treat each other with love and respect. God is love, kind, He is faithful and never late, He is always on time.

27.
MY DARLING CARLOS

Carlos and I still spoke all the time. He was staying at his daughter's house; He didn't feel well and they decided he should stay with her. I felt this was his time to bond with his daughter and grandchildren the way my girls knew him. Carlos always cooked for them all the time.

He came to the house and the four grandchildren were at home. it got late, so I told him he should stay and sleep in the room with my two grandsons. I made sure they were all comfortable and the two granddaughters and I slept upstairs. They were so happy to be in Carlos's company again. The next morning the grandsons were making breakfast. Carlos was in his element; he was so happy when I walked through the door. After this we invited him up to Crystal's house for Sunday dinner. We spoke about everything and anything. We always loved each other's company. Marsha took him back to his daughter's house; we watched him as he got into the house then left.

A few weeks later he called and told me he was in hospital. I told him I would be coming to see him very soon. My heart felt heavy within my chest. I began to breathe deeply. My eyes began to fill up; I couldn't stop the tears. I prayed to God to be with Carlos and please help him get well. I went to see Carlos; I was so happy that he felt much better.

We spoke as usual about what happened. He was in good spirits, and I thanked God. I wanted to Carlos that I had finished with that man but I didn't want him to think because I have finished with him Carlos was second best. I respected him so much. I didn't say anything. I got up tell to pass him something from the table nearby, as I turned around I saw him looking at me. As our eyes met, I noticed a smile on his face. Then he said, "You look really good, I like your boots."

I replied, "Thank you." as I looked over at him, he had a big smile on his face, he was so handsome in my eyes.

Visiting time was up and I had to go. He told me to take care of myself and be careful going home. I replied, "I will". We gave each other a hug and kissed on the cheek.

He then said, "I'll follow you to the door." as he walked me to the door he reassured me, "I will give you a call when I think your home, to make sure you're in safe."

"Ok darling, you take care of yourself, I replied. As he stood looking at me, he said, "Take care, I have to go to the toilet now, speak soon, I will call you to make sure you get in." I left the hospital thinking of Carlos and thanking God for his recovery but I felt sad I couldn't tell him, what I really wanted to tell him.

I called Carlos the following day to see how he was feeling. He told me he was waiting for the result for his heart. I told him to keep me up to date. He reached out, explaining discomfort and an irregular heartbeat, leading him to seek the pacemaker department's assistance. He was told he would be called for an appointment.

Carlos phoned me on the Tuesday and we spoke for a long time on the phone. We talked about his health; he prays because he sometimes feels unwell. I told him to take things easy, to look after himself and to remember that If he ever needed anything I'm still here for him. We ended speaking about the love of God. He told me he is depending on and trusting God for everything.

The next day he rang me, thinking I had called him. I told him I didn't call him and I would call him back later.

Later didn't come. I got a call instead from his daughter's phone saying come on dad come on dad. I then realised that the paramedics were resuscitating Carlos. I couldn't believe what I heard. His daughter told me to come now. I knew, my Carols was in trouble, then I heard Carlos's granddaughter say down the phone, I'm coming for you, aunty. I then didn't know what to do or say. I called Ava and told her to come now. Ava didn't live far from me. I was trying to get my thoughts together but I couldn't think.

I didn't know where my shoes, coat or bag were. It seemed my brain had shut down. I had Marsha's daughter Jessica, who was six. I had to wait for my friend to come to take care of Jessica. Ava (who has been my friend 62 years) came through the door and asked, "Are you feeling ok Vee?"

"Not really, Carlos is not well. I have to go and see what's going on. It doesn't sound good Ava, thank you for coming to look after Jessica." I tried to put my coat on. I didn't know how I got to Carlos's daughter's house. My whole, world had just crumbled.

When I got to the house the door was open. I entered the first room to see Carlos on the floor not breathing and so still. I cried out with unbelief." Oh darling, have you gone and left me, Oh Carlos!", as I cried I couldn't believe what I was seeing. My whole life and world were shaken and broken to see Carlos on the floor. "Oh darling. What am I going to do without you babes?"

Oh, I felt the brokenness, all my dreams are gone. *What am I going to do now?* I felt so much hurt within my being. The hurt in my head felt so heavy, my heart was beating ten to a dozen. I felt my chest, racing and I had to take quick breaths in and out to stop my heart from beating faster. I realised I didn't have any control over the way I felt. I couldn't stop the way I was breathing and the pain that was in my stomach, it was hurting and felt like someone was cutting me open. I felt so lost, not knowing what to say or what to do now.

I stroked his head, his face and lay by his right arm, his daughter was stroking his left hand. I gently kissed him and told him I loved him. I saw people in the room but I didn't and wasn't bothered if they were watching or listening. I lay on his right shoulder holding his arm and then realised he was becoming cold and had to put his hand in a good position. Then I saw Crystal and Sabrina come into the room. I saw my eldest grandson Tristin come through the door, he was crying. I felt so sad because he had such a close relationship with Carlos all his life, and he left, as he couldn't watch Carlos for long.

As I was sitting there watching Carlos, I glanced to see Crystal and Sabrina watching me. Crystal was sitting closer to me and started rubbing my arm. I knew they were also in shock, bewildered with unbelief. My attention went back to Carlos's chest I wanted Carlos to start breathing, I watched, as I was concentrating on his chest, praying for movements up and down. The room was very quiet; you could hear a pin drop. As I looked around the room everyone seemed like they were statues. Everyone was staring at Carlos; he looked like he was just sleeping. I had to close my eyes and open them again; it appeared to me like I was dreaming and any minute I would wake up. Turning my head back to Carlos he was still laying on the floor not breathing.

The tears rolled down my face, I felt sadness and loss, not knowing what to do now. A thought came into my mind is this real, has Carlos really died. It felt so final, I couldn't get my head around it. I began to feel, I was dreaming and would wake up in a minute with Carlos by my side. Looking back, I regret not praying with Carlos, or singing for him as his hearing was the last sense to go in the dying process.

There were a lot of people in the room but it felt like it was only Carlos and I, as I started again stroking his face and his beard. I couldn't focus on anything else. I was praying God please help me at this time, I feel so lost and don't know how to cope with this. Carlos was now getting colder. Still, he was not breathing. It's true my darling has really died. After a while the undertakers came for Carlos's body.

This was difficult to see him being put in a black bag, put on a stretcher to get him to the hearse. I went out of the room and stood outside, whilst they were bringing my Carlos out on a stretcher. I still couldn't believe this. I watched as the undertaker drove away with Carlos's body. This was the worst experience since the death of my dear mum. I said to his daughter I'm going and walked home with Crystal and my granddaughter.

Going home was very difficult; I can't remember how I got home. I couldn't feel my feet beneath me. There was silence, tears, sadness and unbelief that I would never again be able to hug or kiss my darling Carlos. I couldn't have anything to eat or think of anything but Carlos's handsome face and him being alone without me by his side.

I remember praying before bed but can't remember sleeping but I must have because four days after was Christmas and I couldn't do anything. I prayed and asked God to look over us and guide us to get through this day of celebrating your Son coming into the world so we can have life more abundantly. The days went by but it felt like I wasn't really in my body but existing.

New Years came and the same feeling of existing but not being ok and just trying to stay afloat. Bereavement is a time of loneliness for me. I didn't want to be angry with anyone, but felt upset, downcast, in a state, not knowing what to do or say, very quiet. I felt distant from everyone. I was in a place of sorrow and shock. I still couldn't come to terms with the way Carlos died. He rang me the same day around 1.30pm, he asked, "Vee did you ring me? I was unable, to speak to him at the time, as I was with a hair client and replied "Hi, darling, I didn't you know, but I will call you later".

This was the last word I heard from Carlos. I was told that he cooked dinner for his daughter's household and he sat down and died. This reminded me of the last supper, Jesus broke bread and shared it with them, then washed the disciples' feet. Carlos believed in looking after others, not only his own family. He cared for people; he was a very friendly person throughout his life. He looked after and cared for my three children and six grandchildren. He treated them as his own. I loved him in spite, of his faults, just as he also put up with my faults. We loved each other. I had to remind myself of the life we had, that no one can ever take this away from us, not even death because, Carlos believed in God for everything in his life and I will always stay close to our Heavenly Father. So, we will be together again.

Carlos left me to manage his affairs and I did it in love. I made sure his daughter was by my side in everything. I did everything possible to make sure Carlos's request was done according to his wishes. He had a horse and carriage, and a good service. His second eldest daughter Hannah read the eulogy and his niece Estella in the West Indies wrote most of the eulogy (and did it extremely well) me and Carlos' other two daughters added their own tributes, as well as Crystall and Marsha. Three of Carlos's children and two grandchildren were at the funeral. Unfortunately, his son Paul couldn't attend because he wasn't well. Crystal visited his son to make sure he knew, which I thanked her for doing.

The service went well everyone who spoke delivered and did it very well. This would have made Carlos so proud. Even though he wasn't a person to stand up and speak in front of a crowd, he would show his appreciation, reassurance of what others did. I arranged the after do which was a great venue. Everyone acknowledged the effort and organisation, which was put into Carlos's passing. The service was very well organised and the minister spoke well of Carlos. The church was full of family, friends and others who know Carlos. He was very well known in the community.

It took me sometime to mourn Carlos's passing on the 22$^{nd of}$ November 2023. Both of our birthdays were in February, and he was buried on the 29th ^{of} February 2024. I was distraught and felt I couldn't cope. I prayed and asked God to help me to get through the pain and loneliness that I felt, not able to contact Carlos about anything. One year and six months later I still love and miss him terribly. Today I'm in a new season. I still have Carlos's picture in every room. My bedroom has his picture by my bed side and a beautiful picture of Carlos and I close together smiling showing teeth and very happy. This picture reminds me of how we were most of the time. I always thank Marsha for her thoughtfulness, this wonderful throw, it's never off my bed.

Carlos was the one that explained the love and sacrifices God made for me. By giving his Son Jesus Christ to die on the cross, for me and everyone in the whole world. I surrendered my life completely to God. It felt true and real for me, which meant serving a God that never will let me down, ever.

I have tried to understand why Carlos and I were in and out of our relationship so often. As I write this, it becomes difficult to put down on paper. It felt like there was a magnet that draw us together. Even though when our lives were turned upside down, when there was a clear indication that we were single again, we just couldn't help ourselves because we really knew our relationship was real and we could be honest with each other, no matter what the circumstances, or what life throw at us. We both accepted each other knowing that there were safety and acceptance between us in this special relationship. We found each other easy to live with. There were no dramas, when issues, came up we would talk about it, and give them no time to fester, or develop into remorse. We wouldn't argue or speak badly of each other. There was trust, respect, acceptance, we acknowledged our differences, knowing we are very different. We would listen to each other's opinion or agree to disagree. If it was very important we would revisit the issue another time, as life has a way to look difficult and sometime complicated. Our method did work for us; we would find some way to make things right again. We both knew when we were wrong and apologised. We were never too proud to say sorry but waited for the right time to talk about what had happened or said. Now I'm in a new season, where I've asked God to help me to have the strength and guidance to move forward to the future ahead. Life is very special and I know that Carlos would want me to life each day as my last. He is always with me. I speak to him all the time, I can feel his loving presents around me, all I have to do is just think of him. I feel a peace that passes all understanding. I will never forget Carlos and the hope that one day we will see each other again in glory.

Now I'm in a new season, where I've asked God to keep the family close and whatever life throws at us, forgiveness is the key to freedom and peace.

We are a family that love each other and support each other through thick and thin. My mother has always ingrained within me that family is important and we all may have different personalities but as long as we pray together we will stay together. Be kind to each other, and except each other for who we are but do not break up because together we are strong; divided we are weak. I have tried to keep my family close. Watch this space. God is always in control and will help us to win the race.

ABOUT THE AUTHOR

Veronica M. Liburd is a Hairdressing business owner, lecturer, psychotherapist and a debut author. A mother and grandmother, a praying woman of Christian faith who reached the blessed age of 70 in the *year A Better Tomorrow* was published.

www.ingramcontent.com/pod-product-compliance
Lightning Source LLC
Chambersburg PA
CBHW052024070526
44584CB00016B/1887